WOW IN THE WILD

The Amazing World of Animals

By Mindy Thomas and Guy Raz

Illustrated by Jack Teagle

with Mike Centeno

Clarion Books

An Imprint of HarperCollins*Publishers*

Boston   New York

To Rhett and Birdie, for making my life so wild
and full of WOW —MT

To Henry and Bram, the most wonderful wild animals
a dad could ask for —GR

Donya and little Rosie, this is for you —JT

Clarion Books is an imprint of HarperCollins Publishers.

Wow in the World: Wow in the Wild

Copyright © 2022 by Tinkercast, LLC

clarionbooks.com

Library of Congress Cataloging-in-Publication Data has been applied for.
ISBN: 978-0-358-30689-4 (paper over board) • ISBN: 978-0-358-62336-6 (signed edition)

The illustrations in this book were done digitally in Photoshop by Jack Teagle.
Additional illustrations by Mike Centeno and color by Nakata Whittle.
The text was set in Benton Sans.
Cover design by Samira Iravani
Interior design by Abby Dening

Manufactured in Italy
ROTO 10 9 8 7 6 5 4 3 2 1
4500841371

First Edition

CONTENTS

Part V. Creepy Crawlers   152

Part VI. Awesome Amphibians   182

INTRODUCTION
WELCOME TO
WOW IN THE WILD!

Greetings, Human,

Welcome to *Wow in the Wild*! This book serves as your ticket to join us in exploring some of the most wow-worthy animals in the animal kingdom. As your tour guides, we'll introduce you to animals all over the world, from land, air, and sea! A collection of feathered friends, sassy sea creatures, magnificent mammals, stylish reptiles, awesome amphibians, creepy-crawlers, and more! You'll meet animals of all sizes, shapes, and colors, with all sorts of characteristics and adaptations to help them survive in every environment imaginable.

And this is just the beginning. Scientists estimate that there are over 8.7 million species of animals on planet Earth, and most of them have yet to be discovered!

This is where you come in. We hope that you'll find enough wow in these pages to be inspired to explore, follow your curiosity, and become part of the next generation to care for and protect the Earth as a home to all of the wildlife who depend on it . . . including us *human* animals!

The wow in the wild starts . . . NOW. Keep it wild, Wowzers!

Mindy and Guy

Adaptation Station

Animals are full of clever tricks to help protect themselves from hungry predators. These special characteristics, known as adaptations, come in lots of different forms. Adaptations can be specific body parts, body coverings, or even unique behaviors. Let's visit some adaptation stations at the Characteristic Convention to learn more!

CAMOUFLAGE

Colors! Patterns! Blending! Optical Illusions! Get yourself some camouflage and become a master of disguise!

CLAWS

With a menacing manicure like this, you'll be able to claw your way to the top, forage for food, and slash hungry predators who try to eat you!

HOOVES

Enjoy some all-terrain footwear as these high-tech hooves protect your toes! Whether you're a rhinoceros or horse, goat or giraffe, we've got hooves to meet your needs in every shape and size!

HORNS AND ANTLERS

Don't go headbutting without *this* headgear! And if you're thinking about shedding your old antlers before mating season, go right ahead! (We also accept trade-ins.)

ODOR

Let loose and let it linger—that's our motto! Invest in a stink spray that will spook your enemies and last for weeks!

POISON

Got predators? Poison-packed glands are great in a pinch. Just ask me! I'm a sweet strawberry poison dart frog.

SCALY SKIN AND SHELLS

Protect your soft, vulnerable side with a tough exterior! Our scales, shells, and tough skins shield you from oncoming attacks.

SPIT POWER*

Looking to spit oil from your stomach like the fulmar seabird? Then invest in some serious spit power!

*Not recommended for humans.

STINGING

Nine out of ten bees agree that having a sharp stinger is essential to delivering venom to attackers.

TAILS

Are you looking for the convenience of a clean getaway? Then follow the lead of a lizard and get yourself a detachable tail! Surprise and distract your enemies without the fuss of losing blood and guts.

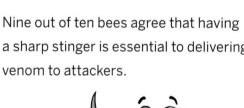

TEETH*

Tear into meat! Take a bite out of bullies! Show your food who's boss!

*Gums not included.

TONGUES

Smell your surroundings, survey the scene, and spot danger snake-style with an extrasensory tongue!

TUSKS

Why hide teeth in your mouth when you can grow them out of your head? Be like an elephant and use your tusks to dig and fight! Or go the way of a narwhal and use your tusk to sense things at night.

FEATHERED FRIENDS

QUIZ: ARE YOU A BIRD?

1. My body is covered in . . .

(A) Scales
(B) Chocolate
(C) Fur
(D) Feathers

2. I am famous for flapping my . . .

(A) Lips
(B) Butt cheeks
(C) Tail
(D) Wings

3. My face features a . . .

(A) Mustache
(B) Mustard stain
(C) Horn
(D) Beak

4. My bones are . . .

  (A) Squishy and cute
  (B) What are bones?
  (C) Spiky (or something else!)
  (D) Partly hollow

5. When I was born I . . .

  (A) Cried like a baby
  (B) Barfed
  (C) Started walking around
  (D) Hatched from an egg

If you answered D to all five questions, CONGRATULATIONS! YOU ARE A BIRD! Birds are the *only* living creatures on earth with feathers. Most, but not all, use their feathered wings and hollow bones filled with pockets of air to help them soar through the sky. Their beaks serve as multipurpose tools that can drill, strain, saw, and crack seeds! But you already know this because YOU'RE A BIRD! And you made that known the second you popped out of that egg laid by your mother.

MOMMA BIRD @MOMBIRD 5m
IT'S A BIRD!

10   5   20

BUT I AM NOT A BIRD!

Oh, you say you're NOT a bird? Well, even better! Come on in and allow us to introduce you to our fine feathered friends.

VANITY AIR PRESENTS:

EIGHT WAYS TO USE YOUR FABULOUS FEATHERS!

HEY, BIRDS! HAVE YOU HEARD THE WORD?
FEATHERS ARE USEFUL FOR MORE THAN MAKING YOU LOOK FIERCELY FANTASTIC!
HERE ARE A FEW WAYS TO MAKE YOUR FABULOUS FEATHERS WORK FOR **YOU!**

1. FANCIFUL FLIGHT!
TWIST AND TURN YOUR TAIL FEATHERS TO FINE-TUNE OR EVEN HIT THE BRAKES ON YOUR NEXT FLIGHT!

2. BUILT-IN RAINCOAT!
WITH THEIR SPECIAL OILY COATING, MOST FEATHERS ARE NATURALLY WATER RESISTANT.
SO GO AHEAD AND FLY THROUGH THE RAIN LIKE NO ONE'S WATCHING! IT'S GOING TO TAKE A LOT MORE THAN A DOWNPOUR TO CRAMP YOUR STYLE!

3. AND AN UMBRELLA!
A HOT TIP FROM ONE OF OUR BLACK HERON READERS: WHEN FORAGING FOR FISH IN SHALLOW WATER ON A BRIGHT SUMMER'S DAY, USE THOSE FEATHERS TO CREATE AN UMBRELLA ABOVE YOUR HEAD AND TAKE THE GLARE OFF THE WATER.

4. CAMOUFLAGE!
FEATHERS ARE DESIGNED TO HELP YOU FIT IN! AND IN SOME CASES, BLEND IN— WITH YOUR SURROUNDINGS, THAT IS. WHEN YOU'RE HIDING FROM WOULD-BE PREDATORS, YOUR BUILT-IN CAMOUFLAGE CAN DOUBLE AS A DISGUISE!
(WE'RE LOOKING AT YOU, OWLS! ONLY WE'RE NOT, BECAUSE WE CAN'T ACTUALLY <u>SEE</u> YOU!)

5. MAKE SOME NOISE!
TWEETING ISN'T YOUR ONLY MUSICAL TALENT. DID YOU KNOW THAT WITH FEATHERS, YOU CAN BE YOUR OWN ONE-BIRD BAND? USE THEM FOR HUMMING, DRUMMING, OR EVEN WHISTLING!

6. MASK SOME NOISE!
TRYING TO TIPTOE YOUR WAY TOWARD HUNTING YOUR NEXT PREY? USE YOUR FEATHERS TO MUFFLE THE SOUNDS OF YOUR WINGS AS YOU APPROACH!

SHHH!

7. DIGESTION!
LOVE FISH BUT HATE THE INDIGESTION THAT COMES WITH IT? TAKE A HOT TIP FROM OUR SEABIRD FRIENDS AND **EAT SOME FEATHERS!** EW?! HOW 'BOUT "OOOH!"? THESE FEATHERS WILL FORM A LINING IN YOUR STOMACH, PROTECTING IT FROM SHARP FISH BONES.

8. HOME DECORATING!
LOOKING TO SPRUCE UP YOUR HUMBLE ABODE? WELL, TAKE A TIP FROM WATER BIRDS WHO USE THEIR FEATHERS TO DECORATE THEIR NESTS. THESE ADDITIONS ARE A FUN, EASY, AND FREE WAY TO ADD A POP OF COLOR TO YOUR SPACE! AND DON'T FORGET, THEY ALSO HELP TO KEEP YOUR EGGS WARM AND PROTECTED.

HOME SWEET HOME

IS THERE ANYTHING FEATHERS <u>CAN'T</u> DO?!

DISCLAIMER: THERE ARE SEVERAL THINGS FEATHERS CAN'T DO; PLEASE DON'T TRY TO DRIVE WITH FEATHERS, MAKE FEATHERS TAKE A TEST FOR YOU, OR ATTEMPT TO MAKE BREAKFAST OUT OF FEATHERS.

WELCOME TO AVIAN AIRLINES

Welcome aboard Avian Airlines! My name's Mindy and I'll be your pilot for today's flight.

And my name is Guy Raz. I'll be your copilot! Today, we'll be flying the Reggie Passenger Pigeon 2000.

Before we take off, we'd like to explain some of the features of this species that make the miracle of flight possible.

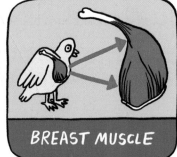

BREAST MUSCLE

If you look to the sides of this airbird, you'll notice a wing on each side.

EXIT

REGGIE PASSENGER PIGEON 2000

LIFT

THRUST

AIR - - - -

The shape of the wing allows air to travel more quickly over the top of the wing than underneath it.

This creates lift and soars our airbird skyward.

But how does that happen, you ask? Well, that is a job for thrust!

You see, on an airplane, thrust is created by turbine engines that propel the plane forward.

MUSCLE POWER

But here at Avian Airlines, thrust is created by our airbird's state-of-the-art breast muscles that help beat those wings up and down, propelling the bird forward.

And we're off! Have a fanciful flight, and thank you for choosing Avian Airlines!

AVIAN AIRLINES

CHECK OUT OUR LATEST FLEET OF FEATHERED FLIERS

OUR FASTEST MODEL: The Peregrine Falcon

FACT: Can dive at speeds of over two hundred miles per hour (320 kph)

LIFESPAN: Up to seventeen years

WINGSPAN: 3.3–3.6 feet (1–1.1 m)

SERVICEABLE ROUTES (HABITAT): All continents but Antarctica

OUR LARGEST MODEL: The Albatross

FACT: Can travel up to five hundred miles (800 km) in a single day. It is the largest seabird on the planet! It barely even flaps its wings when in flight.

LIFESPAN: Up to fifty years

WINGSPAN: 6.5 to 11 feet (1.9–3.4 m)

SERVICEABLE ROUTES (HABITAT): Over-ocean flight paths only

OUR FREQUENT FLIER: The Arctic Tern

FACT: Our Arctic tern airbird racks up about forty-four thousand air miles (or almost two trips around the world) per year. Over the course of its lifetime, it flies the equivalent of the distance from Earth to the moon three times over!

LIFESPAN: Twenty to thirty years

WINGSPAN: 2.7 feet (0.8 m)

SERVICEABLE ROUTES (HABITAT): Arctic Circle to Antarctic Circle

FLIGHTLESS BIRDS

FLIGHTLESS BIRDS NEED LOVE TOO! $1 PER BOOST

NEXT!

UH, MINDY? WHAT IS ALL THIS?

KIWI

JUST GIVING A BOOST TO FLIGHTLESS BIRDS WHO CAN USE ONE?

A BOOST OFF THE GROUND? YOU KNOW THEY REALLY CAN'T FLY.

NO! A BOOST IN CONFIDENCE!

UH.

OH! HERE'S MY NEXT CLIENT. HE'S A CASSOWARY.

FROM THE TROPICAL FORESTS OF NEW GUINEA AND AUSTRALIA?

LOOK, CASSOWARY. YOU MIGHT NOT HAVE WHAT IT TAKES TO FLY. BUT WHO NEEDS FLIGHT WHEN YOU HAVE A SCALY BLUE FACE AND A FLOPPY, COLORFUL NECK? PLUS YOU CAN LAY BIG GREEN EGGS!

NEXT!

IS THAT . . . AN OSTRICH?

LISTEN HERE, YOU BIG PANTLESS THUNDERGOOSE. YOU'RE THE BIGGEST BIRD IN THE WORLD. YOU WERE NEVER MEANT TO FLY. BUT YOU *WERE* MEANT TO DROP-KICK A HUNGRY LION! LOOK AT YOU WITH YOUR TWO-TOED, TURBOCHARGED LEGS AND EYES BIGGER THAN YOUR BRAIN! **NEXT!**

AN EMU?! HOW ARE THESE BIRDS GETTING HERE IF THEY CAN'T FLY?

EMU, YOU'RE A BIG BIRD WITH A TINY NAME. AND SURE, NATURE FORGOT TO TEACH YOU TO FLY. BUT YOU CAN STILL ENJOY THE WIND BENEATH YOUR WINGS AS YOU JUMP SEVEN FEET (2.1 M) STRAIGHT INTO THE AIR! YOU'RE PRACTICALLY THE JACKRABBIT OF BIRDS! **NEXT!**

OH, KAKAPO, YOU WADDLE AROUND, BOUND TO THE GROUND, AND FOR SOME REASON, YOU HAVE THE FACE OF AN OWL. YOU'VE GOT SHORT WINGS, STUBBY LITTLE LEGS, AND ENORMOUS FEET. BUT DO YOU KNOW WHAT MAKES YOU SPECIAL? YOU ARE THE WORLD'S ONLY NOCTURNAL, FLIGHTLESS PARROT! AND NO ONE CAN EVER TAKE THAT AWAY FROM YOU. **NEXT!**

A PENGUIN?! SHOULDN'T YOU BE IN ANTARCTICA?!

WELL, IF IT ISN'T THE FAMOUS FORMAL CHICKEN!

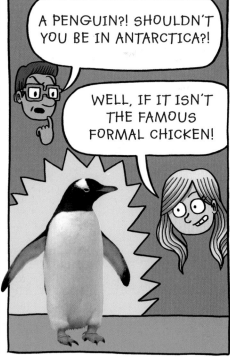

Feathered Friend or Hardcore Wrestler?

- The Blue-Footed Booby
- Hottentot Buttonquail
- The Great Potoo
- The Hamerkop
- Tawny Frogmouth
- The Horned Screamer
- The Chachalaca
- The Moustached Flowerpiercer
- The Cut Throat
- The Yellow-Bellied Sapsucker
- The Kakapo

Answer: They're ALL Birds!

FIGHT!

BIRDS: THEY'RE JUST LIKE US!

Check out this Vogelkop bowerbird creating an art display near his home on the tropical island of New Guinea. Is he hoping that his artfully curated collections of objects will attract a female? Ornithologists (scientists who study birds) say YES!

THEY SHOW OFF!

When it comes to colorful plumage, or feathers, the peafowl knows that *more* is more! Who can compete with a fan like that? Looks like some birds' feathers are too bright to be caged!

You should *see* MY dance moves!

Who needs a pair of blue suede shoes when you've got the dancing feet of the blue-footed booby? Think he's got the moves to attract a mate for life?

Wow. Let's give it up for these two white-browed sparrow-weavers who really know how to draw a crowd! They're one of the few bird species that sing in duet!

IF HUMANS ACTED LIKE BIRDS

I cover myself in ants!

"Anting" is when cardinals and other bird species cover themselves in ants. These ants can be crushed, or alive and crawling! Scientists are still not quite sure why birds do this, but some believe "bathing" in ants help birds to get rid of mites and other parasites. This is not recommended for humans, so don't even think about it.

I hoard acorns!

In late summer and fall, acorn woodpeckers start stockpiling nuts for the winter. They do this by drilling holes in trees, buildings, fence posts, and utility poles, and they use these holes to hide their acorns. Up to FIFTY THOUSAND acorns! They'll stuff each one into its own tiny hole in a single tree, known as a "granary tree."

As it turns out, ravens can sometimes be even more convincing mimics than parrots or even humans! They've been known to copy the sounds of toilets flushing, car engines revving, and humans talking. In the wild, this special skill can be used to lure would-be predators like foxes and wolves when the ravens need help busting open a delicious carcass. Talk about intelligent opportunists!

No need for nuggets—owls prefer to swallow their meat whole! Whether it be a large beetle, a small mouse, or even a tiny bird, an owl can devour its prey in a single gulp! And as we all know, what goes in must come out. So what about those indigestible bits of bones, feathers, and fur? Well, the owl regurgitates them in the form of small pellets. Think of them as little barfy owl nuggets!

HOME TWEET HOME

Grand Nest Designs: Build a Nest That Suits Your Lifestyle

Welcome to Grand Nest Designs. We work with the finest nest builders in the avian world to create custom-built spaces that will hold and protect your eggs *and* your family. From mud to leaves to saliva, here are five of the most fascinating property models available now. Contact us today for a private tour.

THE HAYSTACK

LOCATION: AFRICA'S KALAHARI DESERT

OCCUPANTS: SOCIABLE WEAVERS

TYPE OF ACCOMMODATION: APARTMENT COMPLEX

DESCRIPTION: THIS STRUCTURE HOUSES A HUGE HIVE OF NESTS BUILT TO HOST UP TO FOUR HUNDRED SOCIABLE WEAVERS AT A TIME! WITH ITS THATCHED ROOF, DESIGNED WITH THE HOT DESERT SUN IN MIND, YOU CAN ENJOY COMFORTABLY COOL DAYS AND WARM NIGHTS. YOU'LL FIND THESE NESTS REMAINING IN THE SAME TREES FOR OVER ONE HUNDRED YEARS!

a gardener's dream

LOCATION: AUSTRALIA

OCCUPANTS: MALLEEFOWL

TYPE OF ACCOMMODATION: LANDSCAPED

DESCRIPTION: READY TO THINK OUTSIDE THE TREE FOR YOUR NEXT NEST? WELL, LOOK NO FURTHER THAN THE GROUND! INSPIRED BY THE CRAFTSMANSHIP OF THE AUSTRALIAN MALLEEFOWL AND A COMPOST HEAP, THIS LARGE AND LUXURIOUS MOUND OF A NEST IS TEN TO FIFTEEN FEET (3–5 M) ACROSS AND THREE FEET (I M) TALL. IT'S HANDCRAFTED BY DIGGING A HOLE, STUFFING IT WITH ORGANIC TWIGS AND LEAVES, AND LEAVING THEM THERE TO ROT. THIS PROCESS CREATES A RICH, TEMPERATE COMPOST, PERFECT FOR INCUBATING THOSE SAND-COVERED EGGS THAT YOU WILL LATER ABANDON ONCE THOSE NOISY CHICKS ARE BORN.

A CRAFTER'S DELIGHT

LOCATION: AUSTRALIA, INDIA, AND SOUTHERN CHINA

OCCUPANTS: GOLDEN-HEADED CISTICOLA

TYPE OF ACCOMMODATION: HAND-STITCHED

DESCRIPTION: THE NEEDLE-LIKE BEAK OF THE GOLDEN-HEADED CISTICOLA BIRD HAND-STITCHED THIS NEST BY THREADING SPIDERWEBS AND GRASSES THROUGH BEAK-PIERCED LEAVES. IT SITS JUST TWENTY INCHES (50 CM) OFF THE GROUND.

THE OUTDOOR OVEN

LOCATION: SOUTH AMERICA

OCCUPANTS: RUFOUS HORNERO

TYPE OF ACCOMMODATION: CLAY BASED

DESCRIPTION: RUFOUS HORNERO GOES BY ANOTHER NAME IN SOUTH AMERICA: OVENBIRD! THIS BIRD'S NEST, MADE OF MUD AND MANURE, LOOKS JUST LIKE A CLAY OVEN. AFTER BAKING IN THE SUN, THE STRUCTURE HARDENS, AFFIXING ITSELF TO A BRANCH. (THIS IS ACTUALLY SIMILAR TO THE PROCESS THAT HUMANS USE TO MAKE BRICKS!)

THE STOCKING

LOCATION: CENTRAL AMERICA

OCCUPANTS: MONTEZUMA OROPENDOLA

TYPE OF ACCOMMODATION: SUSPENDED WOODEN STRUCTURE

DESCRIPTION: THE MONTEZUMA OROPENDOLA'S NEST IS MADE FROM TWIGS AND BANANA FIBERS THAT THE BIRD HANGS FROM THE BRANCH OF A TREE. TREES CAN HOLD UP TO 150 NESTS, CREATING A COLONY OF BIRDS! THE FEMALES USUALLY BUILD THE NESTS. IF THE MALE ISN'T PLEASED, HE'LL TEAR IT DOWN AND MAKE HER START AGAIN!

The Lakeside View

LOCATION: SOUTH AMERICA

OCCUPANTS: HORNED COOT, *FULICA CORNUTA*

TYPE OF ACCOMMODATION: HOUSEBOAT

DESCRIPTION: THE HORNED COOT PILES A MOUND OF STONES JUST HIGH ENOUGH TO REACH ABOVE THE WATER LINE. THAT'S WHERE IT BUILDS ITS ABODE OF STICKS AND TWIGS THAT HAS 360-DEGREE VIEWS OF THE WATER.

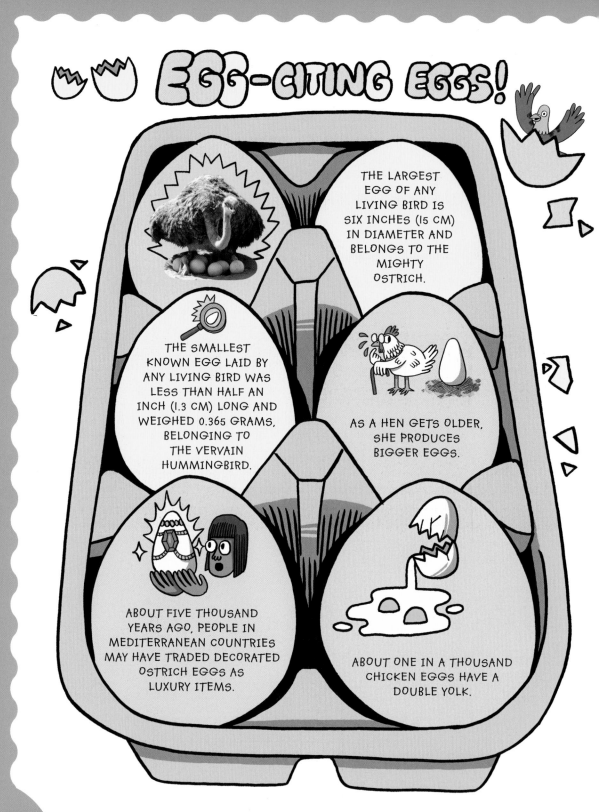

EGG-CITING EGGS!

THE LARGEST EGG OF ANY LIVING BIRD IS SIX INCHES (15 CM) IN DIAMETER AND BELONGS TO THE MIGHTY OSTRICH.

THE SMALLEST KNOWN EGG LAID BY ANY LIVING BIRD WAS LESS THAN HALF AN INCH (1.3 CM) LONG AND WEIGHED 0.365 GRAMS, BELONGING TO THE VERVAIN HUMMINGBIRD.

AS A HEN GETS OLDER, SHE PRODUCES BIGGER EGGS.

ABOUT FIVE THOUSAND YEARS AGO, PEOPLE IN MEDITERRANEAN COUNTRIES MAY HAVE TRADED DECORATED OSTRICH EGGS AS LUXURY ITEMS.

ABOUT ONE IN A THOUSAND CHICKEN EGGS HAVE A DOUBLE YOLK.

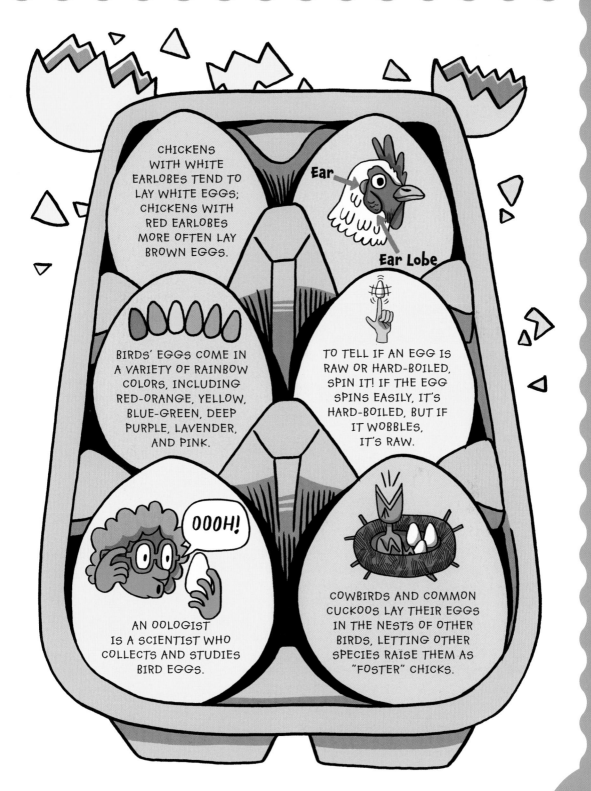

31

THE ANSWER GUY: How do you know if there's a chicken in the egg?

I want to eat this egg, but I'm afraid a chicken will pop out.

Did you get that egg from the supermarket?

Yup.

In that case, your egg is UNFERTILIZED, which means there is no chance of chickens.

Unfertilized?

See, FEMALE chickens, called hens, lay eggs almost every single day. It's a biological cycle that syncs up with the amount of light they receive.

Sorta like my biological cycle of having to pee every morning when the sun comes up?

Uh . . . sort of like that? Anyway, it's only when a MALE chicken, a rooster, is introduced to a group of hens that FERTILIZED eggs are possible.

So the hens are all, "Hooray! A rooster is here! Give us all your fertilizer so we can get some baby chicks in these eggs we're making over here!"?

I don't speak hen.

Me neither.

In any case, the rooster mates with the hens and in the process fertilizes the egg.

So the rooster is putting a baby chicken in the egg?

Well, he's making it possible for a baby chicken to *form* in the egg.

Did I form in an egg?

Well, technically yes, but not the kind you'd find in a store.

So how does a chicken form in an egg?

Well, when this fertilized egg is laid, if it's kept under good incubation conditions, usually warm temperatures . . .

Like under the egg mom's butt?

Well, yes, or even under a heat lamp . . . it will help the chick inside of the egg to grow.

And then what happens??

TA-DA! Chirp Chirp!

MINDY!!!

I got it! The fully formed chick cracks out of the egg and into the world!

So there you have it: no rooster, no chicks.

Just delicious, sunny-side-up eggs! You mind frying this up for me? I like my yolks a little runny.

Fact Snacks

★ Most paleontologists agree that birds are modern-day dinosaurs. Their two-legged theropod ancestors include the *Tyrannosaurus rex* and velociraptors. Many consider the archaeopteryx fossil to be the missing link between dinosaurs and birds.

★ The male peacock (or peafowl), with its tail feathers of up to five feet (1.5 m) long, is one of the largest birds that can fly!

★ Brown thrasher birds can sing more than one thousand songs!

- Bird's nest soup is a common dish found in Southeast Asia, and a main ingredient is BIRD SPIT!

- How to Speak Turkey around the World

  English: GOBBLE GOBBLE
  French: GLOU-GLOU
  Spanish: gluglú

- New Caledonian crows make tools that show preference for the right or left side of their beaks, much as humans show preference for their left or right hands.

- The pileated woodpecker uses its beak to hammer a hole into a tree, then uses its sticky tongue to slurp out ants and termites!

- A woodpecker can peck a tree up to twenty-two times a second!

- Ostriches' eyes are the largest of any land animal.

- The longest recorded nonstop flight by a bird is a whopping eleven days! One bar-tailed godwit flew 7,500 miles (12,700 km) to its home in New Zealand without stopping for food, water, or even rest!

WHAT DO YOU CALL...?

Can you correctly match the bird to its flock?

A) A gaggle of   flamingos

B) A parliament of   hummingbirds

C) A waddle of   geese

D) A gang of   pigeons

E) A murder of   penguins (in water)

F) A flamboyance of   wild turkeys

G) A raft of   crows

H) A charm of   owls

I) A dropping of   chicks

J) A clutch of   penguins (on land)

AFTER WEEKS OF BATTLING IT OUT, WE'RE DOWN TO THE FINAL THREE CONTESTANTS. THIS IS . . .

EAT LIKE A BIRD!

CONTESTANT NUMBER ONE HAILS FROM AFRICA'S GREAT RIFT VALLEY. AND HE'S GOING TO HAVE TO PROVE THAT HE'S MORE THAN JUST PINK PLUMAGE.

FLAMINGO

SO TELL US, WHAT DO YOU HAVE HERE?

HOT BOILING WATER.

AND WHAT DO YOU PLAN TO DO WITH IT NOW? ADD SOME MACARONI? POTATOES?

OH NO, I PLAN TO DRINK IT FOR YOU.

COO?

THE JUDGES

AS IT TURNS OUT, LESSER FLAMINGOS IN AFRICA DRINK NEAR-BOILING WATER THAT THEY GET FROM NATURALLY OCCURRING HOT SPRINGS BECAUSE IT'S OFTEN THE ONLY FRESH WATER AVAILABLE TO THEM. FLAMINGOS ARE ONE OF THE ONLY ANIMALS ON THE PLANET WHO ARE ABLE TO DO THIS! THEY'RE ALSO ABLE TO FILTER OUT A LITTLE SALT FROM SALT WATER AND ELIMINATE IT THROUGH THEIR NOSE.

AHHHHH, SATISFYING!

HAVE YOU CONSIDERED ADDING PAPRIKA?

HARPY EAGLE

AS ONE OF THE LARGEST BIRDS OF PREY ON THE PLANET, THIS CENTRAL AND SOUTH AMERICAN EAGLE HAS ONE BIG APPETITE. AS OUR JUDGES ARE ABOUT TO FIND OUT.

SO, WHAT DO YOU HAVE FOR US TODAY?

LET ME GUESS: A MOUSE? A RAT?

A MONKEY.

OR MAYBE A SLOTH. I HAVEN'T DECIDED YET.

NO! I LOVE SLOTHS!

ME TOO! EVER TRIED 'EM WITH GARLIC AND BUTTER?

HARPY EAGLES LIVE IN THE CANOPIES OF THE RAINFOREST AND OFTEN PREY ON UNSUSPECTING TREE-DWELLING MAMMALS LIKE SLOTHS, MONKEYS, AND OPOSSUMS.

BEING THE TALLEST AND LARGEST BIRD BY FAR IN OUR FINAL THREE, THE OSTRICH MIGHT BE ABLE TO SHED SOME LIGHT ON A LIFE HACK THAT'S HELPED IT TO REACH SUCH IMPRESSIVE HEIGHTS.

OSTRICH

YOU BETTER GET STARTED, MR. OSTRICH. THE TIMER IS RUNNING AND ALL I SEE ON YOUR WORKBENCH IS A BUNCH OF ROCKS.

THAT'S CORRECT.

WELL, YA BETTER GET TO IT!

I'M DONE.

WHAT?

ROCKS FOR DINNER. OLD FAMILY SECRET . . . THEY'RE GREAT FOR DIGESTION.

CAN I GET YOU SOME DIPPING SAUCE TO GO WITH THOSE ROCKS?

WHEREAS MOST ANIMALS (LIKE YOU HUMANS) HAVE TEETH TO HELP GRIND UP AND DIGEST FOOD, MOST BIRDS DON'T HAVE THIS LUXURY. SOME BIRDS, LIKE OSTRICHES, INGEST ROCKS THAT RUMBLE AROUND IN THEIR BELLY, BREAKING DOWN THEIR BIGGER MEALS.

LIKE A BLENDER!

Barf Break!

- Penguin parents barf food into their baby chicks' mouths.

Barf is just a fancy word for "regurgitate"!

- Eurasian roller bird babies barf up a stinky-smelling orange liquid as a defense mechanism against predators. Once they're covered in their own barf, they become less appetizing as a snack.

- Owls barf up neat little pellets that are tightly packed with undigested bits of everything they eat. If you were to peek inside one, you'd find all sorts of treasures: hair, bones, fur, frogs, and more!

But don't take our word for it! You can buy your own owl pellets and dissect them to see for yourself!

★ WILD THINGS ★

HELP WANTED

Delivery Pigeon

THE INTERNATIONAL PIGEON POSTAL SERVICE

JOIN AN ORGANIZATION WITH A LONG, RICH, AND STORIED HISTORY! WITH OVER TWO THOUSAND YEARS OF SERVICE, WE PRIDE OURSELVES ON DELIVERING LONG-DISTANCE MESSAGES ON TIME AND IN ONE PIECE!

THE IPPS IS LOOKING FOR A DEDICATED PIGEON OR ROCK DOVE TO JOIN OUR WORLDWIDE FLEET OF HOMING PIGEONS, INCLUDING THOSE ACTIVELY WORKING IN PARTS OF EUROPE AND ASIA TODAY!

YOU'LL BE JOINING A LONG LINE OF SERVICE BIRDS THAT WERE KNOWN AS THE ORIGINAL "AIRMAIL."

REQUIREMENTS: A KEEN SENSE OF DIRECTION WITH THE ABILITY TO MEMORIZE COMPLEX IN-FLIGHT ROUTES.

APPLY TODAY!

MILITARY DOLPHIN

ARE YOU LOOKING FOR A WAY TO SERVE YOUR COUNTRY, SEE THE WORLD, AND EAT ALL THE TUNA AND MACKEREL YOU CAN STOMACH? THEN MAYBE YOU SHOULD CONSIDER A CAREER WITH THE US NAVY!

SINCE 1959, THE US NAVY'S MARINE MAMMAL PROGRAM HAS BEEN ENLISTING BOTTLENOSE DOLPHINS AND CALIFORNIA SEA LIONS TO HELP PROTECT SAILORS AND MARINES, BY DETECTING UNDERWATER THREATS IN THE OPEN SEA.

WE WANT <u>YOU</u> TO JOIN THIS ELITE UNIT.

ARE YOU A DOLPHIN READY TO TAKE YOUR ECHOLOCATION SKILLS TO THE NEXT LEVEL?

ARE YOU A SEA LION WITH EXCELLENT VISION AND AN EYE FOR DETAIL?

ARE YOU A DECENT SWIMMER?

APPLY TODAY!

TAKE ONE

1-800-SPLASH
1-800-SPLASH
1-800-SPLASH
1-800-SPLASH
1-800-SPLASH

LAND-MINE-DETECTING RAT

ARE YOU A RAT WITH A LITERAL NOSE FOR JUSTICE?
THE NONPROFIT ORGANIZATION APOPO IS NOW RECRUITING
FOR THEIR GLOBAL ARMY OF MINESWEEPING RODENTS,
AND WE WANT YOU—AND YOUR SENSITIVE SCHNOZ—
TO JOIN OUR TEAM!

THIS JOB WILL REQUIRE YOU TO SNIFF OUT TWO THOUSAND
SQUARE FEET (186 M²) OF DANGEROUS LAND MINES IN JUST
THIRTY MINUTES—A TASK THAT WOULD GENERALLY TAKE
A HUMAN MINESWEEPER FOUR <u>DAYS</u> TO COMPLETE!

IF HIRED, YOU CAN EXPECT TO UNDERGO UP TO
NINE MONTHS OF TRAINING, AND BE REWARDED WITH
SNACKS THROUGHOUT THE PROCESS.

**SO . . . ARE YOU READY TO MAKE A DIFFERENCE IN
MINE-INFESTED COMMUNITIES?**

APPLY TODAY! VISIT WWW.APOPO.ORG FOR MORE INFO!

ALL RAT CANDIDATES FOR THIS JOB MUST WEIGH NO MORE THAN
3.3 POUNDS (1.5 KG); ANY MORE, AND WE RUN THE RISK OF SETTING OFF
THE LAND MINES WE'RE WORKING TO DEACTIVATE.

ULTIMUTT GUIDE DOG

DO YOU HAVE FOUR PAWS, A WAGGLY TAIL, AND THE DESIRE TO SERVE? THEN SIGN UP TODAY AND LEARN TO BE THE ULTIMUTT GUIDE DOG!

AS A GUIDE DOG, YOU'LL BE TRAINED IN THE SKILLS NEEDED TO SERVE BLIND OR VISUALLY IMPAIRED HUMANS ALL OVER THE WORLD!

JUST LOOK AT ALL THESE NEW SKILLS YOU'LL LEARN!

- STICKING TO A DIRECT PATH

- HELPING YOUR HUMAN AT CROSSWALKS

- IGNORING DISTRACTIONS (SUCH AS CATS, SMELLS, AND OTHER EXCITING THINGS)

- BEING ABLE TO TELL WHAT OBSTACLES YOUR HUMAN WON'T BE ABLE TO WALK THROUGH AND FINDING AN ALTERNATE PATH AROUND THEM

DON'T HESITATE! BE A GOOD DOG AND APPLY TO BE A GUIDE DOG TODAY!

REPTILE
STYLE

DEAR BABY REPTILES,

Welcome to the world! While you are each one of at least eleven thousand different and unique reptile species, the world will soon be categorizing you into groups of crocodiles, alligators, snakes, lizards, turtles, and tortoises. And while we celebrate your differences, it's important to remember the traits you all share in common! Allow us to take a moment to help you get to know yourselves and each other, before you make your way into the wild.

I. You are covered in either scales or scutes, and both will serve to protect you throughout your life journey.

Scales   **Scutes**

2. You will shed your skin! Just remember, there is always more skin to be had.

3. You will be deeply affected by the temperature of your environment. Because you are cold-blooded ectotherms, your bodies are of little help when it comes to warming up or cooling down. This means you must find your own outside sources of warm sun or cool shade.

5. When it's cold, you will get lazy! Okay, maybe not *lazy*, but because your metabolism slows down when you are cold, you will become *inactive*.

7. Your ancestors hung out with dinosaurs! Take these bragging rights with you into the world.

Now go forth, little reptiles, and share your wow with the world!

In cold blood,

Mindy and Guy

4. You will not be able to sweat. This is perfectly natural. For you.

6. From the moment you were born (most likely from an egg), you were ready to hit the ground running! Have patience, little ones. Some of you may live for the next hundred years or more.

SSSSSSSSCALES ARE MADE UP OF OVERLAPPING LAYERS OF SKIN.

AND SCUTES ARE THE THICKENED HORNY OR BONY PLATES FOUND ON A TURTLE'S SHELL OR THE BACK OF A CROCODILE!

Relaxation Spa

FOR THE COLD BLOODED

Are you constantly cold?
Yes!
Are you tired of your body temperature getting in the way of enjoying your life?

Then you should snake a break and join us at the . . .
Reptile Retreat Center, a relaxation spa for the ectothermic!

As a cold-blooded ectotherm, we know how important it is for you to depend on the outside world to control your inner body temperature.
And that's why we provide amenities to help with all of your thermoregulation needs.

Warm up in the hot sun on any of our signature resting rocks!

Cool down in a shady pool of chilled water.

Our resort offers these tried-and-true methods to help bring your body temperature back down after you've laid in the sun for a tad too long.

So what are you waiting for? Beat your metabolism down to the Reptile Retreat Center! And for 10 percent off, tell 'em Wow in the World sent ya!

All animals (including humans) are either ectothermic (cold-blooded) or endothermic (warm-blooded). Ectothermic animals, like reptiles, amphibians, fish, insects, and arthropods, have body temperatures that get hotter or colder depending on their environment. An ectothermic animal might lie in the sun to warm up, or find a shady spot to cool down.

Endothermic animals, like mammals and birds, keep a constant body temperature even when the temperature of their environment changes. They're also able to help control their temperatures, for example, by shivering to keep warm and sweating to cool off.

THE COLD-BLOODED CREW

Are you an ectotherm or an endotherm? How can you tell?

Season's Greetings to Our Friends and Family!

Well, another year has gone by, and for this familia Reptilia, that means *out* with the old, *in* with the new! And with that, we shed a few more layers of skin, just as our great great-great-great-great-great-great-great-great-grandparents might have done 315 million years ago. (*We took an ancestry test this year and found out that SOME of us have lineages that are older than DINOSAURS! Can you believe it?*)

Speaking of dinosaurs, ol' Turtle and Tortoise are still going strong and doing everything they can to avoid extinction. In fact, Great-Great-Grandma Tortoise celebrated her 150th birthday this year! We all went down to South America to party in the Galápagos Islands (*ooh la la!*), and oh, we had a HOOT! Ate all the grass and leaves we could stomach! Which wasn't much for some of us who prefer eating antelopes and zebras. (I'm looking at you, Alligator and Crocodile!)

Alligator and Crocodile spent another year being constantly confused for one another. I mean, sure, they both have long snouts and tails and mouths full of peg-like teeth. And yes, they both have nostrils and eyes on the tops of their heads—but clearly the similarities end there! Anyone who has ever spent some one-on-one time with Alligator would know that she has a short, broad, U-shaped snout, whereas Crocodile *clearly* has a V-shaped mouth! And you'll NEVER see those two swimming together . . . well, except maybe in Florida. Alligator is very particular about her "fresh" water. (Can you believe we caught her in a human's toilet this year?!) Crocodile also enjoys fresh water, but he usually likes to dabble in a little salt water too.

For those of you wondering about the snakes, you'd be happy to know that they're still slitherin' around and scaring people—despite the fact that most of them are completely harmless to humans. I mean, c'mon! They can't chew, they have no limbs, they can barely see or hear, and they can't even hunt or digest their food unless the temperature is just right!

Well, that's all for now. On behalf of the entire familia Reptilia, we hope that you have a festive holiday season.

Later, gators!

The Familia Reptilia

HIDE-AND-SEEK

Chameleons are masters of disguise, and it all comes down to their superpowered color-changing technique!

A chameleon's skin is covered in teeny-tiny cells called nanocrystals. These nanocrystals reflect light at different wavelengths depending on how many of them are clustered together. And by relaxing or exciting their skin, chameleons are able to control whether these cells are spaced far apart or close together, which makes different combinations of yellow, blue, red, and orange. This is how they control the color of their skin!

Ready to play a little chameleon-style hide-and-seek? See if you can spot the six most common chameleons hiding in this picture!

Jackson's chameleon

Usambara pitted pygmy chameleon

Veiled chameleon

Bearded pygmy chameleon

Panther chameleon

Spectral pygmy chameleon

Potty-Mouthed Turtles!

The Chinese softshell turtle pees through its mouth. In fact, when scientists were studying these turtles, they kept them in dry boxes and gave them puddles to dip their heads into. They found that the turtles could hold their heads underwater for up to one hundred minutes and pee about fifty times more urine through their mouths than through their rear ends! And speaking of rear ends, when some turtles hibernate, they essentially breathe . . . through their butts!

HEY! DO YOU MIND?

Fact Snacks

★ Some cave-dwelling salamanders have almost completely lost their eyesight!

★ Some cobras can squirt venom up to six feet (1.8 m)— longer than one hockey stick.

★ In 2014, a cobra bit a chef in China twenty minutes after its head had been CUT from its body!

EYE TEST

- At a hair salon in Germany, you can get a neck massage from a four-foot (1.2-meter) python!

- Paleontologists discovered a prehistoric supercroc that was almost as long as a city bus and may have weighed as much as three tons (2,700 kg)!

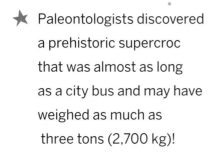

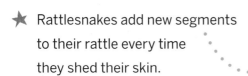

- Rattlesnakes add new segments to their rattle every time they shed their skin.

- Australia's thorny devil lizard "drinks" water by absorbing moisture from wet sand through its skin.

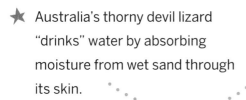

- Twenty-one of the twenty-five most venomous snakes in the world live in Australia.

- A group of turtles is called a "bale."

BALE

- A tangled knot of rattlesnakes is called a "rhumba."

WHAT TO EXPECT WHEN YOU'RE EXPECTING... A BUNCH OF BABY CROCODILES

Congratulations! You're expecting a bunch of baby crocodiles! Here are a few tips on the care and feeding of your little bundles of joy.

BURY THEM! We know it sounds bonkerballs, but if you're going to give your little hatchlings a fair shake at life, you're going to have to bury the eggs they're currently growing in. You can bury them underground or make a little mounded nest near the water! Whatever you do, just make sure they're hidden from predators.

FILL UP YOUR PATIENCE TANK!
It's going to take anywhere from eighty to ninety days for these hatchlings to bust out of their eggs and into the world. So get yourself a calendar and a couple of crossword puzzles. You might be here awhile.

KNOCK KNOCK! SQUEAK SQUEAK!

It's SHOWTIME! When your crocs are about to hatch, they'll start making tiny squeaking noises from *inside* their eggs. This is your cue to dig up the nest, crack open the eggs, and pop those babies into your mouth to carry them to the water, stat!

IT'S TIME TO GET UP NOW!

KNOCK KNOCK!

DON'T FORGET TO FEED THEM!

Your little hatchlings are about the size of a candy bar, but this doesn't mean they should be *eating* a candy bar. You'll want to round up as many small snails and fish, insects, and tadpoles as you can find. These will be your babies' favorite foods for a while.

THANKS, MOM!

And that's it! No bibs to put on or diapers to change, just a bunch of baby crocodiles that won't mature until they're at least around ten to fifteen years old.

So saddle up, it's going to be a WILD ride!

I'M AN AMERICAN ALLIGATOR, AND HERE ARE FIVE THINGS YOU SHOULD KNOW ABOUT ME:

HI!

1. I have so many teeth! (We're talking seventy-four to eighty teeth at a time!) And when they fall out or I wear them down, my mouth fills with new teeth! Not to brag, but I could go through as many as two thousand teeth in my lifetime.

2. I can't stop growing! You think I'm big now at nine feet (2.7 m) long? Well, just you wait until I'm an old grandpa alligator! By then, I could measure up to fifteen feet (4.6 m) and weigh as much as a thousand-pound (450-kg) baby grand piano!

3. I am VERY VOCAL! I also have no vocal cords. So how do I do it? Well, I suck air into my lungs, then blow it back out! This creates a loud, roaring bellow that I can use to declare my territory, let others know when I'm unhappy, intimidate my competitors, and even find a mate. I'm also known to growl, hiss, and make a coughing sound called a chumpf.

4. I'm kind of a big deal! I contribute to my ecosystem by digging my signature "alligator holes," which act as small ponds, holding water during the dry season and providing habitat for other animals. Do they ever thank me? Nah. It's just my way of giving back to the community.

5. I'm a big charmer! At the start of every spring, I'll perform some loud bellows to attract a female mating companion. I'm also known to blow bubbles and slap my head on the surface of the water. And if you're looking for a snout or back rub, I'm your gator!

And on his farm he had an alligator . . .

E-I-E-I-Ohhhh!

SCALY STARS: IT'S A TALENT SHOW!

IT'S TALENT TIME IN THE REPTILE ROOM!

LET'S BRING ON THE SCALY STARS OF THE SHOW!

GREEN ANACONDA

FOR MY TALENT, I WILL HUG YOUR GUTS OUT! I'M THE LENGTH OF FIVE TEN-YEAR-OLDS HEAD TO FOOT, SO THERE IS PLENTY OF ME TO WRAP AROUND YOU! AS A CONSTRICTOR, I COME FROM A LONG LINE OF HUGGERS. IT'S JUST WHAT WE DO!

TOO TIGHT! TOO TIGHT!

WOULD YOU RATHER WATCH ME SWALLOW AN ALLIGATOR?

NEXT!

DESERT TORTOISE

FOR MY TALENT, I WILL SHOW OFF MY BIG BLADDER!

OKAY, LET'S SEE IT!

WELL, I CAN'T TAKE IT OUT OF MY BODY, BUT IF YOU THREATEN ME, THEN I SUPPOSE I CAN EMPTY IT ON THIS STAGE. IT'S HOLDING ALMOST 40 PERCENT OF MY BODY WEIGHT IN PEE AND OTHER STUFF.

NO THANKS! WE'LL, UH, TAKE YOUR WORD FOR IT.

61

★ WILD THINGS ★

WOW COMICS CLUB PRESENTS

THE ANIMAL AVENGERS SERIES

Oh! The sea cucumber has special fibers that can turn from rigid to a softer state on command!

THE SHAPESHIFTING SEA CUCUMBER

PREDATORS DON'T STAND A CHANCE!

NON-ESSENTIAL ORGANS: EJECT AND DISTRACT!

WATCH IN AMAZEMENT AS IT TRANSFORMS ITS BODY FROM ROCK SOLID TO SUPER SQUISHY!

So that's how it's able to squeeze into tight spaces and escape predators!

THE ELECTRIC EEL
SHOCK JOCK OF THE DEEP

BUILT IN BATTERIES (BASICALLY)

50 TIMES MORE VOLTAGE THAN A CAR BATTERY

SHOCK WAVES OF UP TO 600 VOLTS!

When it's threatened or attacking prey, it will discharge all of its electrical power at once! Talk about a shock to the system!

Wow! That would really pack a punch!

Unbelievable! Whenever it's sick or hurt . . .

It transforms all the cells in its body back to their baby stage!

THE IMMORTAL JELLYFISH
THE FOUNTAIN OF YOUTH

GROW UP? NOT ME! POOF!

NOW I'M A BABY!

IT TRANSFORMS ALL THE CELLS IN ITS BODY BACK TO THEIR BABY STAGE!

THE **FLEA** READY TO LAUNCH!

JUMPING 200 TIMES ITS OWN BODY LENGTH IN A SINGLE BOUND!

That would be like me trying to jump to the top floor of the Empire State Building!

Imagine the amount of energy stored in those tiny flea legs!

Is this all true?!

Oh yeah, the mantis shrimp has two appendages called dactyl clubs. These come in handy when it wants to stun its prey or break free from an aquarium.

THE MANIACAL **MANTIS SHRIMP** FISTS OF FURY

ONE SWING AND WATER **BOILS**!

PACKS A PUNCH MORE POWERFUL THAN A SPEEDING BULLET!

THE MIMIC OCTOPUS

MASTER OF DECEPTION AND DISGUISE

NOTHING TO SEE HERE, VENOMOUS SEA SNAKE! I'M ONE OF YOU!

WATCH IT CHANGE THE COLOR OF ITS SKIN TO BLEND INTO ITS SURROUNDINGS

MOST FAMOUS IMPERSONATOR IN THE OCEAN! SEE IT HIDE A PART OF ITS BODY TO DISGUISE ITSELF AS A SEA SNAKE.

I heard its body is covered in cells called chromatophores, which help it to change into any color!

And I heard that it impersonates other sea creatures to ward off danger!

LYREBIRD
MASTER MIMIC

IT'S A SCIENTIFIC MYSTERY!

- KOALAS!
- DINGOES!
- CAR ALARMS!
- CHAINSAWS!
- RINGING PHONES!
- CRYING BABIES!
- LASER GUNS!

THE **TINY TARDIGRADE**
EXTREME SURVIVOR!

TAKE THAT!

HOW TOUGH?

- EXTREME TEMPERATURES? BRING 'EM ON!
- RADIATION!
- BOILING LIQUIDS!
- THE VACUUM OF SPACE (WITH NO PROTECTION)!

She's so cute and tiny!

She's also indestructible!

Wow. I damaged my elbow and all I got was this cool scar!

THE SALAMANDER
REGENERATION OF LOST LIMBS

DAMAGED OR LOST LIMBS? NEVER FEAR! THE MACROPHAGES ARE HERE! WITH THE HELP OF THESE IMMUNE CELLS, SOME SALAMANDERS HAVE THE SUPERHERO ABILITY TO SPROUT NEW LIMBS!

MAGNIFICENT MAMMALS

ARE YOU A MAMMAL?

Take this quiz to find out!

1. Are you covered in hair or fur?

2. Do you have a one-piece lower jaw?

3. Does your internal body temperature generally stay the same no matter where you are?

4. Do you breathe air?

5. Does each member of your family get two sets of teeth in their lifetime?

If you answered YES to all of these questions, *you* must be a mammal!

Mammals are everywhere. We can be found on every continent, both on land and underwater, and have the amazing ability to adapt to all types of ecosystems. Mammals can be massive, like the blue whale, or as minuscule as the bumblebee bat. And when it comes to movement, mammals are known to walk, run, swim, jump, hop, climb, and dive, and in one case, even fly.

Out of the 5,400 different known mammal species on earth, there are a few key traits that all mammals share:

Hair—sometimes in the form of fur or whiskers

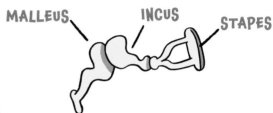

MALLEUS   INCUS   STAPES

Three tiny middle-ear bones

A hinged jaw (like YOURS!)

Mammary glands for nursing their young

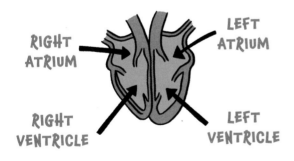

RIGHT ATRIUM   LEFT ATRIUM

RIGHT VENTRICLE   LEFT VENTRICLE

A four-chambered heart

In addition to this, most mammals are warm-blooded endotherms, and many will have just two sets of teeth over a lifetime.

WHAT'S IN YOUR POUCH?

Marsupials, mammals commonly known for having pouches or folds of skin to hold their babies, are usually found in the "Land Down Under," known as Australia. The word *marsupial* comes from the Latin word *marsupium*, which means "pouch." However, despite their namesake, not all marsupials have pouches. The short-tailed opossum, for example, has no pouch at all!

We checked in with some of our favorite marsupial pals and asked the question: What's in *your* pouch?!

I like to keep babies in my pouch. Usually around fifteen of them at a time! This keeps my *opposable thumbs* free to raid trash cans for food at night!

Her "opposable thumbs" are actually more like "opposable TOES."

The Virginia opossum, or common opossum, is the *only* marsupial found in the United States and Canada.

But all the babies leave behind is poop and pee?

Just like pregnant humans, pregnant kangaroos have ways of preparing for the arrival of a new baby. Through an act known as "preening," a kangaroo will make room in her pouch for its new occupant by cleaning out everything left behind by the last one.

JUST MAKING SOME ROOM!

Exactly. And the mom cleans it all out with her tongue!

Well, as you can see, I have a little "mini me" inside my pouch. And since my pouch is backward, opening toward my butt, I also keep a strong sphincter muscle in there to keep her from falling out.

KOALA

Not only do I keep my joey, Joey, in here, but I also have a milk dispenser so he can eat and drink. This frees me up for doing other things, like being the largest and fastest marsupial on the planet!

RED KANGAROO

In my pouch, you'll find an assortment of crumbs, candies covered in hair, magnifying goggles, a shrink wand, a hammer, a hamster, some shrimp, and . . . a diaper?

CAN YOU CORRECTLY MATCH THE MAMMAL WITH ITS BABY NAME?

MAMMAL	BABY NAME
A. Goat	1. Joey
B. Hedgehog	2. Whelp
C. Kangaroo	3. Kid
D. Mouse	4. Hoglet
E. Otter	5. Puggle
F. Platypus	6. Pinkie

Answers: A–3, B–4, C–1, D–6, E–2, F–5

HOW TO PLAY DEAD (OPOSSUM STYLE!)

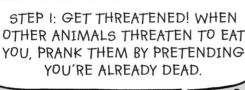

STEP 1: GET THREATENED! WHEN OTHER ANIMALS THREATEN TO EAT YOU, PRANK THEM BY PRETENDING YOU'RE ALREADY DEAD.

STEP 2: HISS AND BARE YOUR TEETH UNTIL YOUR BODY INVOLUNTARILY SHUTS DOWN, PUTTING YOU INTO A NEAR-COMA-LIKE STATE.

HISS HISS

STEP 3: AMP UP THE FREAK FACTOR BY FALLING OVER ON YOUR SIDE, WITH YOUR EYES AND MOUTH WIDE OPEN.

STEP 4: RELEASE A STINKY FLUID FROM YOUR BUTT. (IF IT MAKES YOU SMELL LIKE ROTTEN MEAT, YOU'RE ON THE RIGHT TRACK.) THE POINT IS TO MAKE YOURSELF SMELL SO DISGUSTING THAT YOU'LL SCARE YOUR PREDATOR AWAY.

STEP 5: KEEP DOING THIS UNTIL YOUR BODY DECIDES IT'S HAD ENOUGH "PLAYING POSSUM" FOR ONE DAY. THIS COULD TAKE UP TO FOUR HOURS, SO MAKE SURE YOU HAVE A LOT TO THINK ABOUT WHILE YOU'RE FAKING YOUR OWN DEATH.

EGG-LAYING MAMMALS

The platypus and the spiny anteater (echidna) are monotremes, or rule-breaking rebels when it comes to mammal classification. Like all other mammals, they:

★ Produce milk: YEP!

★ Nurse their babies: CHECK!

★ Have hair: YOU BETCHA!

★ Hear as the result of the vibrations of three middle-ear bones: YASSSSSSS!

After that, their differences take a turn for the wild.

★ Give birth to live young: NOPE! WE LAY EGGS, BABY!

★ Have milk-producing mammary glands: NOPE! WE HAVE LITTLE SWEATY MILK PATCHES INSTEAD!

Monotremes also go back . . . *waaaaaay* back. In fact, both the platypus and the echidna have been around in one form or another for the past two hundred million years—they even lived alongside dinosaurs. The only monotremes still in existence today live in Australia and New Guinea.

The word *monotreme* comes from the Latin word for "one hole." Monotremes have one hole called the "cloaca" that they use for just about everything.

GET YOURSELF A CLOACA! THE HOLE THAT DOES IT ALL!

WITH THE CLOACA, YOU CAN:
• POOP OUT OF IT!
• PEE OUT OF IT!
• REPRODUCE OUT OF IT!

I want a cloaca! Can you eat out of it too?

Never eat where you poop.

Many animals live in close-knit groups, or societies, with other animals of their species. These are known as social animals. Social animals live, work, and cooperate with one another to help the group survive, thrive, and reproduce. See if you can match the following social mammals with their group names.

ANIMALS

A. Apes

B. Bats

C. Camels

D. Cats

E. Elephants

F. Foxes

G. Gorillas

H. Kangaroos

I. Lemurs

J. Monkeys

K. Oxen

L. Rhinoceroses

M. Weasels

N. Hippopotamus

GROUP NAME

1. Band

2. Conspiracy

3. Shrewdness

4. Crash

5. Gang

6. Colony

7. Team

8. Clowder

9. Caravan

10. Parade

11. Troop

12. Mob

13. Skulk

14. Bloat

Answers: A—3, B—6, C—9, D—8,
E—10, F—13, G—1, H—12, I—2, J—11,
K—7, L—4, M—5, N—14

Wait, we ARE mammals!

MAMMALS: THEY'RE JUST LIKE US!

THEY TAKE CARE OF THEIR KIDS!

This polar bear mama has been taking care of her cub for the last two years. She protects him from other polar bears and teaches him how to hunt and how to eventually take care of himself. When he starts to wander, she makes a clicking sound to call him back to her.

THEY GET MAD!

Look at these angry llamas sticking out their tongues and spitting at one another! What do you think they're brawling about?

THEY'RE TICKLISH!

Not only is this rat ticklish, but it's also LAUGHING! So why can't we hear its joyous squeals? Well, that's because rats laugh at a high-pitched frequency that cannot be detected by human ears. But rat-tickling scientists have been able to translate their giggles, and the results will make you LOL!

THEY HAVE SECRET LANGUAGES!

These elephants are communicating at a sound frequency that's so low, humans and other animals can't even hear it! And what's even more bonkerballs is that other elephants can hear their calls from miles away. Researchers observing elephants in the wild found that these giant mammals use hundreds of secret vocal sounds, signals, expressions, and gestures to communicate with one another.

MONKEY BUSINESS

Let's eavesdrop on these spunky monkeys as they share the scoop on what makes them the unique primates we know and love.

The more excited I get, the brighter my face! Also, I have snack pouches in my cheeks!

I pee on my hands to wash my feet!

What's the secret to a long-lasting relationship?

We mate for life!

Yeah, we're life partners.

Always show affection for your other monkey. You can do this by grooming them . . .

Or holding hands, cuddling, intertwining tails . . .

Lip smacking!

Okaaay.

We get it! You're prime-mates!

You can hear our screams from three miles away!

I smile when I'm angry!

Oftentimes, monkeys will grin as a sign of aggression.

WE ARE NOT MONKEYS! MONKEYS HAVE TAILS! WE DO NOT!

Actually, MOST—not ALL—monkeys have tails.

Chimpanzees Are a Lot Like Humans!

Genetically speaking, chimpanzees are our closest relatives in the entire animal kingdom. Since they share almost 99 percent of our DNA, it's no surprise that chimpanzees have more in common with us humans than we realize:

- They use sticks to scratch their backs!

- They pat each other on the back!

- They hug and kiss!

- They laugh when tickled!

- They create tools to help them eat!

- They recognize themselves in the mirror!

- They share!

- They show their feelings!

INTERVIEW WITH A VAMPIRE... BAT

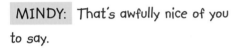

MINDY: Hey, so thanks for coming all the way from a dark cave in South America to talk to me!

VAMPIRE BAT: It's no problem. I love humans.

MINDY: That's awfully nice of you to say.

VAMPIRE BAT: But not as much as I love cows, pigs, horses, and . . . uh . . . oh! Birds!

MINDY: Well, I love all those animals too.

VAMPIRE BAT: The blood of livestock—it's exquisite! MMM-MMM-MMM!

MINDY: Right, because you're a blood-sucking vampire bat.

VAMPIRE BAT: FALSE! Why does everyone say that about me? I am not going to suck anyone's blood!

MINDY: Whew! That's a relief.

VAMPIRE BAT: Instead, I will puncture my victim's skin with my sharp, tiny teeth.

MINDY: Uhh . . .

VAMPIRE BAT: And then I will LAP up the blood with my tongue.

MINDY: I'm not sure that's any better.

VAMPIRE BAT: Ah, but I am so GRACEFUL. The last cow I bit didn't even wake up!

MINDY: Well, that's good, I guess.

VAMPIRE BAT: See, I'm very efficient. I have a special sensor on my nose that helps me to locate the best and bloodiest spot on my victim.

MINDY: Ew.

VAMPIRE BAT: But I'm also very generous. Sometimes I'll barf a little blood into my bat friends' mouths.

MINDY: WHY WOULD YOU DO SOMETHING LIKE THAT?!

VAMPIRE BAT: Because in exchange, they'll give me a bath. It's called "grooming."

MINDY: So you barf blood into other bats' mouths in exchange for a spa treatment? Pretty sure that's not how generosity works.

VAMPIRE BAT: Pretty sure it is.

MINDY: Pretty sure it's not.

VAMPIRE BAT: . . .

MINDY: Okay, one final question: Should I *be* scared of you?

VAMPIRE BAT: Well, like I said, I prefer cows and such to humans, but I AM full of a disease called rabies, so . . .

MINDY: So no hugs?

VAMPIRE BAT: I AM A WILD ANIMAL!

MINDY: I'll take that as a NO?

VAMPIRE BAT: NEVER hug a wild animal!

MINDY: High-five?

VAMPIRE BAT: You're missing the point.

89

COMMUNICATE LIKE A MAMMAL!

Hello! Hola! Bonjour! Konnichiwa! And welcome to the Wow in the World Communication Course.

Looking to pick up a new skill and become a better communicator? Always wanted to learn a new language but never knew where to start? Well, lucky for you, the Wow in the World language course is now available.

Choose from a variety of human languages, such as:

★ Spanish   ★ Italian   ★ French   ★ Baby

We also cover a wide variety of other mammalian languages, such as:

Whale

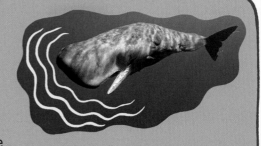

Learn to communicate from some of the best communicators on the planet: WHALES! Whales know that their unique communication skills are key when it comes to tracking down food, navigating oceans, and maybe even identifying friends from strangers. Register today and receive:

Your own unique name that only a whale can say!

Not only do whale pods have their own dialects that they use to communicate with one another, but those dialects are like foreign languages to whales in other pods!

The secret to "SECRET LANGUAGES" of whales!

Scientists believe that because sperm whale songs and communications are so unique, they may have individual names that other whales call them!

Wolf

Wolves know that the secret to survival is clear communication. In this course, you will learn how to express your intentions and emotions through a series of howls, growls, whines, whimpers, and yips.
This course is essential to keeping your "wolf pack" in check!*

*Recommended for families.

Through this four-week wolf-speak course, we'll cover:

Wolf growling: How to show dominance and scare off intruders. *Translation: "Back off!"*

Pack howling: How howling together in chorus builds social bonds and makes everyone feel part of the pack. *Translation: "We're all in this together."*

Wolf barking: How to warn others in the pack about an oncoming threat. *Translation: "Watch out!"*

Wolf whining: How to express your emotions with others in your pack. *Translation: "Let me be real with you for a second . . ."*

Dolphin

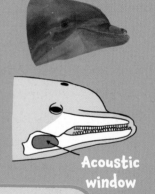

Learn to communicate underwater over long distances by using low-frequency sound waves. Highly skilled dolphins will share their signature whistles and low-frequency clicks to have you spinning your own dolphin tales in no time!

Acoustic window

Although dolphins might not have ears that stick out like us humans, they're able to hear their neighbors through a special structure in their jaw called an acoustic window.

Prairie dog

And say hello to our latest language pack: prairie dog! The language of these pop stars is one of the most complex animal languages we've been able to decode so far. Thanks to research on the Gunnison's prairie dog from Northern Arizona University, we're able to offer our most complete mammal language program to date!

In this course, you'll learn:

1. A variety of prairie dog warning calls, including ones for coyote, domestic dog, human, and hawk.

2. How to construct descriptive sentences like a prairie dog, e.g., "A large, rectangle-shaped dog with brown fur is coming," or "Here comes a short human wearing a brown T-shirt who is also hairy."

3. Because researchers know that certain yips from the prairie dogs translated to descriptions about oncoming predators, they were able to work with computer scientists to develop an algorithm that converts the prairie dogs' vocalizations into English. That's right: if you can't be bothered going through our language course, we do also offer a translation service that will help you communicate with your little prairie friends.

So what are you waiting for? Sign up today and learn the calls and communication *secrets* of the mammal kingdom!

If you add them all up, rodents make up nearly half of all the mammals found on earth! And you can find them pretty much everywhere, from dry land and fresh water to your own attic and kitchen floor! In fact, if you wanted to escape the presence of rodents altogether, your best bet would be to travel all the way to Antarctica, a frozen land where no wild rodents dare to roam.

PYGMY JERBOA

Rodents come in all sizes and shapes too: from the teeny-tiny pygmy jerboa to the giant guinea pig relative the capybara. But rodents are most known for their self-sharpening front teeth! These chompers give many of them the power to gnaw through just about anything and everything, from wood to wire, and they never stop growing!

WOW! THAT'S a Rodent?

When you hear the word *rodent*, what animals come to mind? Mice? Rats? Squirrels? Let's get to know some of the unsung heroes of the rodent world.

THE AFRICAN CRESTED PORCUPINE

The African crested porcupine is the world's best-armed rodent, and these quills are made for stabbing. Predators beware: when threatened, this porcupine gets prickly, charging backward into its enemy with its sharp, hollow quills.

CAPYBARA

The capybara is the world's largest rodent. It hails from the swamps of Central and South America, can grow to the size of a small pig, and can hold its breath underwater for up to five minutes when trying to escape an enemy.

SOUTH AFRICAN SPRINGHARE

The South African springhare might look like a cross between a tiny kangaroo and a rabbit, but it's actually—neither! It's a rodent.

BEAVER

The beaver is the largest rodent in North America, weighing up to sixty pounds (27 kg)! It's famous for its swimming and dam-building skills, and its versatile paddle-shaped tail not only helps it to work its way

through water, but also serves as a tool for communicating with other beavers. But perhaps its biggest wow factor is its specialized GUTS, which are equipped for digesting tree bark!

CHOMP!

THE NORTH AMERICAN SOUTHERN FLYING SQUIRREL

It's a bird! It's a plane! It's a . . . North American southern flying squirrel? Folds of stretchy skin "wings" help this rodent glide between trees, traveling almost 150 feet (46 m) in a single flight!

GAZ-ELLE MAGAZINE

TREND ALERT: HORNS!

POLL: HIGH-HEELED HOOVES?

STRIPES VS. SPOTS

HOW TO DRESS FOR YOUR HABITAT

TAILS! A TOP 10 LIST

QUIZ: ARE YOU A UNICORN?

THE HOTTEST TRENDS IN THE MAMMALIAN KINGDOM
FROM PREHENSILE TAILS TO BLUBBER IN WHALES!

TREND ALERT: HORNS!

HORNS. Permanent. Pointy. Protruding.

Horns are made up of bony cores that have been hardened by layers of a fibrous protein called keratin. They're super versatile and never go out of style!

So get yourself a pair of horns and use them to:

INTIMIDATE YOUR ENEMIES!
This is often done to gain territory, dominate another male in the herd, or win a mate.

WHAT ARE YOU LOOKING AT?

FIGHT FOR DOMINANCE!
Show your species you've got what it takes to LEAD!

FORAGE FOR SNACKS! Highland cows have been known to use their long horns to sift through snow to find edible plants.

BE COOL! Horns can help an animal to regulate its body temperature.

DECORATE YOUR HOME! The male wildebeest uses his horns to scrape the bark off nearby trees to impress females.

Horns come in all shapes and sizes, and are ALL beautiful. Let's travel around the world to see what horns we can find.

Indian Rhinoceros

While horns are traditionally worn in pairs, this is one rhinoceros who broke the mold—a one-horned wonder!

Asian Water Buffalo

The longest horns of any living animal belong to the largest bovine, the Asian water buffalo. These massive horns can grow up to five feet (1.5 m) long!

OSSICONES

Giraffe

Yes, even giraffes are sporting horns—although they may not look like what you'd expect. Giraffe horns are called ossicones and are covered with skin. And while both males and females have them, only males use them to fight with other males.

4.9 feet

Oryx

The oryx uses its horns as swords to fight in epic battles between males. These horns can grow up to 4.9 feet (1.5 m) long and come in a variety of different shapes:

★ Straight!   ★ Curvy!

★ Curly!   ★ Spirally!

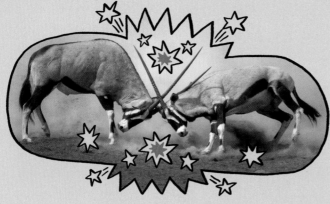

Musk Ox

The male musk ox sports two bones that combine to form a band across its forehead that's known as a "boss."

Bighorn Sheep

This sheep's horns are so spectacular, it's named after them! Male horns can weigh up to thirty pounds (14 kg), and the size is considered to be a symbol of rank in the sheep's herd.

Unicorn

The unicorn horn is spiralized, sparkly, and made out of myth-wrapped imagination!

I'd just like to point out that unicorns are not actually real.

Not with that attitude they're not!

PARADE OF POOPERS

Wombats

The wombat is a pudgy little marsupial native to Australia. It lives in underground burrows, can run up to twenty-five miles per hour (39 kph), and has a set of teeth that never stop growing. It also poops in *cubes*! In fact, it's the only animal on the planet whose poop regularly comes with ninety-degree angles.

I POOP CUBES!

Baby Koala

A newborn koala must prepare its body for eating tough and fibrous eucalyptus leaves. It does this by building up helpful bacteria in its gut by eating poop right out of its mom's butt. It's called pap feeding, and it's totally normal . . . if (and *only* if) you are a koala.

I EAT MY MOM'S POOP!

Why do animals behave like animals?

Sloth

The sloth spends the majority of its time in the treetops of South and Central American rainforests. However, once a week, like clockwork, it makes the exhausting trek from its safe treetop canopy to the rainforest floor, making itself vulnerable to predators. Why? To POOP.

This habit has puzzled biologists for decades, mainly because sloths have such low energy. Getting themselves to the rainforest floor would be the energy equivalent of you deciding to run a weekly 5K race just to poop!

So why go through so much effort when one could just as easily poop in the trees? Nobody knows for sure, but one hypothesis is that going down to the ground to poop gives the moths living on the sloth's back a place to lay their eggs, which would help moths continue their life cycle.

I RISK MY LIFE EVERY TIME I POOP!

Sloths are covered in moths and algae??

Yep! The sloths give them a place to live, and in return the algae camouflages the sloth from predators. It's a symbiotic relationship.

Sperm Whale

When threatened by a predator, the sperm whale will poop out an explosion of fecal matter (that's a fancy word for poop) and use its billowing tail to stir it into the surrounding water. This creates a poop cloud that can help disguise its escape. Talk about an emergency evacuation!

POOP EXPLOSION!

Giant Panda

Giant pandas eat roughly thirty pounds (14 kg) of food every single day. And what goes in must come out . . . in the form of LOTS AND LOTS OF POOP, sometimes fifty times per day! Why? Well, it turns out the giant panda isn't great at digesting food. Despite having eaten bamboo almost exclusively for the last two million years, its gut is only able to absorb about 17 percent of the food it eats in a day. The rest comes right back out its rear end!

I POOP ABOUT 50 TIMES A DAY!

That's a high-fiber diet!

ANIMALYMPIC CHAMPIONS

Tallest, smallest, fastest, slowest: let's meet the world record holders of the mammal kingdom!

World's Fastest Land Mammal: Cheetah

TEAM: Africa

> That's faster than my Ferrari!

FACT: This big cat is built for speed. Known for its powerful acceleration and short-distance sprinting, the cheetah can go from zero to forty-five miles per hour (72 kph) in three seconds flat.

> SHOUT-OUT TO MY LONG LEGS, FLEXIBLE SPINE, AND STURDY TAIL FOR KEEPING ME BALANCED.

> Mindy, you drive an ice cream truck!

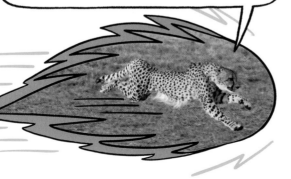

World's Slowest Mammal: Three-Toed Sloth

TEAM: Central and South America

FACT: Living life in the slow lane, the three-toed sloth tops out at high-speeds of 0.15 miles per hour (0.24 kph). In fact, it could take a whole minute for the sloth to move the length of one adult human. This pokey pacer is so slow, algae grows on its fur, giving it a natural disguise from predators as it spends its days hanging in the treetops. If you ever come upon a sloth in the wild, give it some privacy. It's likely just made a journey to the rainforest floor for its weekly bathroom break!

World's Tallest Mammal: Giraffe

TEAM: Africa

STOP ASKING ME IF I PLAY BASKETBALL!

FACT: It's not called the "skyscraper of the savanna" for nothing! The tallest giraffe in the world clocks in at a whopping eighteen feet, eight inches (5.7 m) tall, with a neck stretching to more than seven feet (2.1 m)! This impressive height gives the giraffe an all-you-can-eat advantage when it comes to the buffet of tree leaves that other herbivores can't stretch to reach.

World's Smallest Mammal: Pygmy Shrew or Etruscan Pygmy Shrew

YOU GONNA EAT THAT?

TEAM: North America

FACT: Tied with the bumblebee bat for the title, the pygmy shrew is officially considered the world's smallest mammal by mass. This pocket-size predator has a body length of 1.5 to 2 inches (3.8–5 cm) and weighs less than a paper clip, but don't let its small stature fool you. The pygmy shrew must eat six times its body weight daily just to stay alive!

World's Biggest Land Mammal: African Elephant

DO MY EARS LOOK LIKE THE CONTINENT OF AFRICA TO YOU?

TEAM: Africa

FACT: Weighing up to fourteen thousand pounds (6,350 kg) and standing up to thirteen feet (4 m) at the shoulder, this heavyweight champion weighs as much as two limousines and is twice as tall as basketball champ Michael Jordan! And animals can breathe a sigh of relief in knowing it won't want to eat them. The African elephant is a salad-loving vegetarian.

HUGE!

And by salad, we're talking three hundred pounds (136 kg) of leaves, grasses, tree bark, and fruit each day!

You can find more than three thousand seeds in the African elephant's daily dung!

World Champion of Blowing Other World Champions Out of the Water: Blue Whale

TEAM: All of the oceans (except for the Arctic)

GOLD MEDALS:

Largest Animal on the Planet

That's longer than an eighteen-wheeler truck!

★ Up to 105 feet (32 m) long

Heaviest Animal on the Planet

That's heavier than *seventeen* school buses combined!

★ Up to four hundred thousand pounds (180,000 kg)

Biggest Baby on the Planet

Introducing our big bundle of blubber

Born via water birth

Twenty-six feet (7.9 m) long

Six thousand pounds (2,722 kg)

We love you more than all the fish in the sea!

Loudest Animal on the Planet

★ Blue whales can wail at up to 188 decibels when communicating in the ocean.

Biggest Appetite on the Planet

★ Eats up to eight thousand pounds (3,600 kg) of krill in a single day!

That's louder than a jet plane!

Eight thousand pounds?! That's as heavy as some African elephants!

THE FUR BALL

Mammals are the only animals in the entire animal kingdom that have fur and hair.

Hair and fur can help mammals keep warm and, in some cases, blend in and camouflage themselves from potential predators.

Let's explore some of the hottest looks in furry fashion!

Highland Cattle

FASHION MEETS FUNCTION!

Fringe is *in,* according to this rustic breed of Scottish cattle. But this thick coat is more than just an iconic fashion statement; it's also a highly functional fashion choice. The Scottish highlands are known for harsh winters,

where temperatures rarely rise above forty degrees Fahrenheit (4 degrees C), and snow can fall up to one hundred days of the year or more. This long, luxurious fur keeps the cattle warm while looking cool.

Comes in a variety of stunning colors: red, black, yellow, and silver!

Bactrian Camel

SEASONABLY WARM AND CAMEL COOL!

When it comes to fur, are two coats better than one? They are if you're a Bactrian camel! Hailing from the deserts of eastern Asia, this mammal makes sure its fur is always in season. They prepare for cold winters by growing a thick coat in the fall. And when spring comes peeping through, it's out with the old and in with the new! The Bactrian camel drops its winter coat in patches to make room for a lighter, thinner coat of fur for the spring!

Hedgehog

SPIKY STYLE!

OUCH!

This hedgehog is sporting a stiff, sharp, modified version of hair called quills. Quills are made out of keratin, the same material that hair and fingernails are made of. This prickly coat is not only fashion-forward, it's also a lifesaver at fending off hungry predators.

Fact Snacks

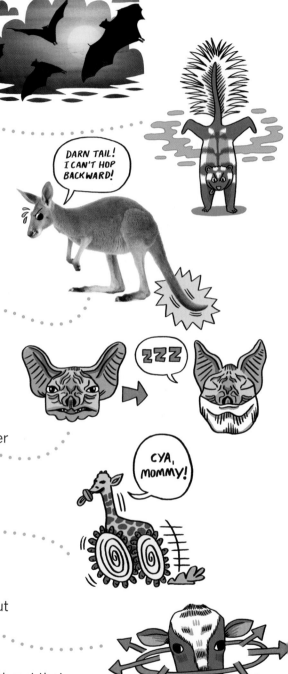

★ Bats are the only mammals that can truly fly.

★ When threatened, the eastern spotted skunk will move into a handstand before it sprays.

★ Cheetahs have the ability to change direction midair when chasing down their prey.

★ Kangaroos can't hop backward. Their long, muscular tail acts as a third leg and gets in the way.

★ Wrinkle-faced bats pull their skin over their face while they sleep.

★ Newborn giraffes can run an hour after they're born.

★ Domestic cows have almost 360-degree panoramic vision without even moving their heads.

★ Pandas have a thick coating in their throat that prevents them from getting bamboo splinters.

SAY CHEESE!

LET'S MEET SOME OF THE ANIMAL KINGDOM'S MOST SMILEY MAMMALS.

QUOKKA

"I'M SMILING BECAUSE
I'M HOT! I'M PANTING AND
THIS IS JUST HOW
MY MOUTH IS SHAPED."

DOLPHIN

"THIS IS NOT A SMILE.
IT'S AN ANATOMICAL ILLUSION,
AND I CAN'T DO ANYTHING
TO CHANGE IT."

DRILL MONKEY

"I GRIN TO KEEP THINGS CHILL WHEN I MEET
OTHER MONKEYS. THIS IS HOW I KEEP THE PEACE."

THE PINK PAGES

The Flamboyant Flamingo

It's perhaps the most famous pink animal on the planet, but you might be surprised to know that the flamingo is not born pink! In fact, when a baby flamingo hatches, it's actually gray. It isn't until the first couple of years of its life that its pink coat starts to appear. This is the result of a special pigment found in the algae, insect larvae, and small crustaceans that the flamingo eats!

Looks like somebody's been eating ALL the shrimp!

Did you know that as of 2019, there were only about two hundred pink iguanas left in the wild?

Yeah! And they all live on one small volcano in the Galápagos Islands. Talk about a pinky paradise!

The Pink Iguana

While the pink iguana might appear to have pink skin, the truth is, its skin is actually TRANSPARENT! A lack of pigment in its skin allows you to see the blood underneath, giving it that electric pink glow.

The Pink Dolphin

While this pink dolphin might look like a cotton-candy-colored cutie, don't be fooled! The male Amazon River dolphin gets his pink hue from . . . FIGHTING! Scientists believe the pink skin on these dolphins is the result of scar tissue that forms from rough-and-tumble fights. The pinker the skin, the tougher the male and the more attractive he is to females.

Pink Poop

The Adélie penguin of Antarctica is literally pooping out pinky pride! Their pink poop is due to a special pigment in the food they eat, a pinkish crustacean known as krill. And because these penguins live in large colonies that poop together, this pink poop is visible from space!

The Domestic Pig

While not all piggies wear pink, the domestic pig has become one of the most famous pink animals on the planet! Originally, all pigs were black, brown, hairy, and WILD. But when a genetic mutation resulted in the first pink pig, humans became so enchanted by the hue that for generations they specifically bred and domesticated this species. Hence the pink piglets we see today!

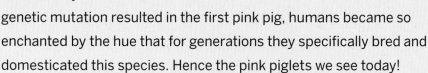

Salmon

Sometimes it's what's pink on the *inside* that counts! That's certainly the case for salmon: silver on the outside but pink through and through. This is due to pigments in its diet called carotenoids that give the salmon's inner flesh its electric rosy glow.

Bargibant's Pygmy Seahorse

When you're a pygmy seahorse, pink is more than the color of your body, it's a way of life! This tiny master of disguise camouflages itself to match its home on pink fan corals. It wasn't even discovered until a researcher found it while studying coral in a lab!

The Elephant Hawk-Moth

One of the fastest flying insects is also one of the pinkest! The green and pink elephant hawk-moth uses its colors to attract mates by night while hiding among the bright pink blossoms of its favorite fuchsias by day!

The Naked Mole-Rat

This blushing beauty has been described as everything from a tiny walrus to a bratwurst with teeth! The naked mole-rat gets its pinkish-gray tones from its wrinkly, almost translucent skin and its mostly hairless body.

The naked mole-rat queen is the only member of the colony that produces babies.

The Pink Fairy Armadillo

The smallest species of armadillo is also the pinkest! This is because the blood vessels of the pocket-size pink fairy armadillo show through its thin shell. But (like other fairies) don't count on spotting one in the wild! The pink fairy armadillo lives almost its entire life underground, burrowing through the earth, gobbling up bugs and other creepy-crawlies and nibbling on plant matter. We should also note that this fairy does not have wings and cannot fly.

The Pink Robin

A plump, pink-belled wonder from the Land Down Under! Australia's male pink robin weighs little more than a pencil but is a brightly hued standout in the sky.

SASSY SEA CREATURES

Welcome to the under(water) world! Here you'll find some of the over thirty-two thousand species of fish, plus an array of sea-dwelling invertebrates such as sponges, octopuses, sea stars, oysters, lobsters, and much, much more! It's a dark but colorful world of creatures unlike any you'll ever find on land. Let's take a deep dive inside!

SIX SIGNS YOU MIGHT BE A FISH

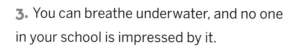

1. Full-time underwater living is for you.

2. No one has ever accused you of *not* having a backbone.

3. You can breathe underwater, and no one in your school is impressed by it.

4. You don't need legs, arms, or artificial flippers to help you swim.

5. Your skin is covered in scales and/or slime.

6. At birth, you had as many as a thousand siblings, all of whom probably hatched from eggs.

FISHTORY
CLASS IN THE
SCHOOL OF FISH

It's a pun on HISTORY!

About four hundred million years ago, in the ancient oceans of our planet, sea life was abundant. But the creatures found in those waters looked a lot different from the sea creatures today. Thanks to fossil records, paleontologists have been able to create pictures of what these sea creatures looked like before they became extinct. Let's take a peek at some of the most famous fishy ancestors.

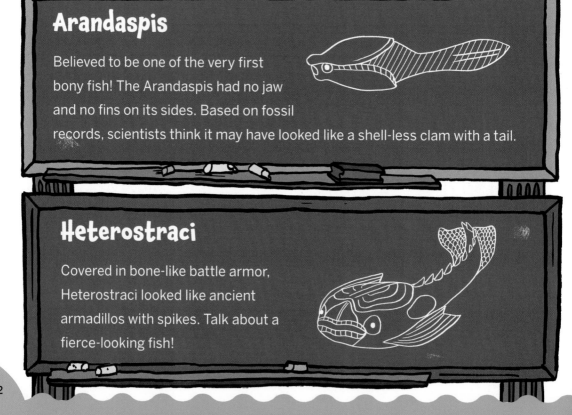

Arandaspis

Believed to be one of the very first bony fish! The Arandaspis had no jaw and no fins on its sides. Based on fossil records, scientists think it may have looked like a shell-less clam with a tail.

Heterostraci

Covered in bone-like battle armor, Heterostraci looked like ancient armadillos with spikes. Talk about a fierce-looking fish!

Osteostraci

With helmets that looked like horseshoes, these armored fish might have battled hungry predators.

Placoderm

One of the first fish to have a jaw! These predatory fish used their powerful jaws to dominate the deep!

Galeaspida

Sure, there were many fish in the sea, but how many of them sported helmets with SWORDS?

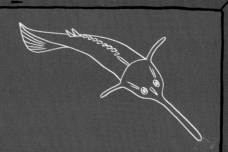

Thelodonti

Built like a tank with razor-sharp teeth, the thelodonts sported scales instead of heavy armor.

LOUSE GOT YOUR TONGUE?

IN THE GULF OF CALIFORNIA, THERE LIVES A CERTAIN TYPE OF TONGUE-EATING, BODY-SNATCHING LOUSE KNOWN AS THE **CYMOTHOA EXIGUA**.

EWWW!

LET'S WATCH IT DO ITS THING!

STEP 1: THE HUNGRY LOUSE SPOTS A BEAUTIFUL RED SNAPPER.

STEP 2: IT DECIDES TO CRAWL INSIDE OF IT BY ENTERING THROUGH ITS GILLS.

STEP 3: IT LATCHES ONTO THE TONGUE.

STEP 4: IT EATS ALMOST THE ENTIRE TONGUE.

NOM NOM

STEP 5: IT REPLACES THE TONGUE **WITH ITS OWN BODY.**

WHAT?!

DON'T WORRY, THE LOUSE LIVES HAPPILY EVER AFTER AS A FULLY FUNCTIONING **NEW** TONGUE FOR THE FISH!

UH . . .

YEAH! IT HELPS THE RED SNAPPER TO GRIND FOOD AGAINST THE TINY TEETH ON THE ROOF OF ITS MOUTH AND EVERYTHING!

AAAH!

YOU MIGHT WANT TO PUT THAT THING AWAY!

STAR:

NO. 1 FOR SEA STAR NEWS

ALL BEAUTY AND NO BRAINS?
A SEA STAR EXPLAINS!

CONFESSION TIME:
I AM NOT A FISH!

USE YOUR COLORS TO
DAZZLE PREDATORS!

READ HOW THIS SEA STAR LOST
ITS ARMS AND GAINED A WHOLE
NEW LIFE!

THIS CHOCOLATE CHIP STARFISH
LOOKS GOOD ENOUGH TO EAT.
BUT SHOULD YOU?

SEE WITH YOUR
ARMS!

COLD BLOODED
WARM BLOODED
NO BLOODED?

FIVE WAYS TO WEAR YOUR
STOMACH ON THE OUTSIDE

MAKE A FISH FACE!

THE CAMERA LOVES YOU!

RED-BELLIED PACU: SAY CHEESE! This mostly vegetarian piranha is known for its humanlike teeth and crushing bite that can crack stubborn seeds and nuts. However, if it runs out of its main food supply, the red-bellied pacu *will* devour other fish. Add it as a terrifying twist to your aquarium!

GOBLIN SHARK: This little underwater cutie is a descendant of a family of sharks that lived during the Cretaceous period, 125 million years ago. The goblin shark is easily recognizable by the adorably long and skinny snout protruding from the top of its head and razor-sharp teeth extending from the bottom. The goblin shark can thrust its jaw out of its face, latching onto prey before reeling it in for a tasty seafood treat!

NORTHERN STARGAZER: Ever imagine what you'd look like if your face was on the top of your head instead of, well . . . on your face? When it comes to the stargazer, that's the case! With an enormous mouth and big, bulging eyes sitting on top of its head, this ferocious fishy buries itself in the ocean floor for a little game of hide-and-seek with unsuspecting prey. And that's not all! The stargazer also comes with two venomous spines above its pectoral fins and the power to zap any predators with a surprising electric shock.

WONDERFUL, DARLING!

It's so cute, I'm gonna barf!

BLOBFISH: It's what's inside that counts! Scientists think that two thousand–plus feet (more than 600 m) under the ocean surface, there lives an ordinary fish with an ordinary face. This fish thrives on the deep-sea floor, but when you bring this unusual creature up to the surface, things take a turn for the weird. Once removed from the high pressure of the deep ocean, the blobfish stops looking like a fish and starts looking like a big, swollen pile of pink slime with a grumpy humanlike face. In fact, the blobfish was once voted the unofficial Ugliest Animal on Earth by the Ugly Animal Preservation Society! Congratulations, blobfish, on being number one!

SHRIMP COCKTAIL PARTY

HERE ARE SOME FUN CONVERSATION STARTERS TO USE TO HELP YOU MIX AND MINGLE AT YOUR NEXT SHRIMP COCKTAIL PARTY!

I LOVE YOUR SEE-THROUGH BODY! YOU REMIND ME OF A GHOST!

YEAH, IT'S REALLY JUST A BUILT-IN DISGUISE TO HELP ME HIDE FROM PREDATORS WHEN I'M BACK AT SEA.

HELLO! I'M SKELETON SHRIMP

SO, ARE YOU HERE WITH YOUR WHOLE CREW OF CRUSTACEANS?

YEAH, WE PRETTY MUCH DO EVERYTHING TOGETHER: EAT, TRAVEL, BREED . . . I NEVER GET ANY "ME" TIME, YOU KNOW?

SO, WHAT'S YOUR FAVORITE FOOD?

UH . . . I GENERALLY ONLY EAT, LIKE, ALGAE AND ROTTING ORGANIC MATTER OFF THE OCEAN FLOOR.

129

FISH OR MAMMAL?

Not everything that lives in the ocean is a fish! These vast waters are full of all kinds of animals, including mammals, some of which people often confuse with fish. Can you tell the difference between a fish (like a shark) and a mammal (like a whale)?

WHALE SHARK

ORCA

BOTTLENOSE DOLPHIN

SPERM WHALE

GREAT WHITE SHARK

NURSE SHARK

Answers: Fish: Whale shark, Nurse shark, Great white shark; **Mammal:** Sperm whale, Bottlenose dolphin, Orca

Train yourself! Learn the differences! Impress your friends!

FISH

★ Fish swim by moving their tail side to side.

★ Fish have gills so they can breathe underwater.

★ Almost all fish are ectothermic (cold-blooded) animals. This means that they rely on their environment to help control their inner body temperature.

MARINE MAMMALS

★ Marine mammals swim by moving their tail up and down.

★ Marine mammals do not have gills. They have to come to the surface to breathe.

★ Marine mammals are endothermic (warm-blooded) animals. This means that they are able to help control their own inner body temperature.

FRIGHTENING FRILLS

WITH LOOKS THAT COULD GILL!

STARRING: THE FRILLED SHARK

With a serpent-like body and over twenty-five rows of razor-sharp, three-pronged teeth—three hundred teeth in all!—the frilled shark looks less like a modern-day fish and more like a living fossil of ancestors that were around one hundred million years ago. Not that you'll ever see one up close. The elusive frilled shark lives in a place so deep underwater, humans have rarely seen it with their own eyes.

The deep-sea dragonfish makes its home in one of the most hostile environments on the planet, more than 1,600 feet (488 m) below the ocean surface. In this underwater twilight zone, the waters are largely still and sunlight is nonexistent. It is here that this eel-like, fang-toothed deep-sea fish lurks around in search of a snack. To light its way, the dragonfish uses a glowing organ called a photophore to locate and lure unsuspecting prey into its deadly and jagged jaws.

With the largest teeth in the world in comparison to its body size, the fangtooth lives up to its name. In fact, this ferocious fish's teeth are so big, it can't even close its mouth all the way without special protective pouches. And if you're a fish, crustacean, or cephalopod, you'd better beware. The fangtooth is ready and waiting to open its jaws wide and suck you inside. Good luck trying to wriggle free from the barbed jaws of one of the deepest-living fish that's ever been discovered.

With a supersized, expandable mouth that's bigger than its body, the gulper eel is in search of its next BIG GULP. And its prey doesn't even know it's coming. Disguised by its black, velvet-like exterior and armed with a whip of a tail, the gulper eel moves through the dark waters of the deep like a stealthy assassin. Sea creatures of all shapes and sizes had better beware!

THE BIG GULP

MORE THAN A MOUTHFUL

STARRING: GULPER EEL

THE COSMIC JELLYFISH

UFOHHHHHHHHHHHH WOW!

With a luminous, see-through body and two sets of tentacles, this creature looks like an extraterrestrial UFO! It was first discovered in 2017 by a remotely operated underwater vehicle controlled by researchers at the National Oceanic and Atmospheric Administration (NOAA). It was spotted in a remote part of the Pacific Ocean nearly 9,800 feet (3,000 m) below sea level. No underwater aliens were detected during the mission.

SHARK TOOTH FAIRIES

Have you always dreamed of spending time inside of a shark's mouth?

I know I have!

Well, this is the closest you're ever gonna get to it!

So come on in!

Most sharks have between five and fifteen ROWS of razor-sharp teeth! And since a lot of these teeth have no root system to hold them in place, they're poppin' out left and right!

But don't blame it on bad dental hygiene. Some shark teeth are even naturally covered in fluoride, making them completely cavity-resistant!

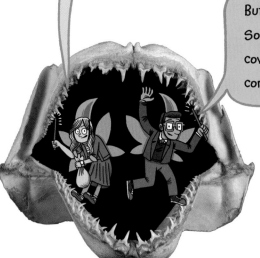

Sharks NEVER have to go to the dentist and yet they STILL don't eat candy!

For a lot of sharks, once a tooth falls out, the tooth behind it is ready to move forward to fill its place in the shark's mouth.

It's a real tooth factory in there! "Second row . . . you're up!"

And a whole new tooth pops up in the back row to make up for the one lost.

Unlimited supply of teeth!

# SHARK BITES

Baby shark, doo doo doo doo do do:
a baby shark is known as a PUP!

A group of sharks
is called a SHIVER.

Sharks were swimming the seas
before dinosaurs ever roamed
the earth!

SLEEP IS FOR WIMPS!

Sharks rest,
but they don't sleep
the way we humans do.

The hammerhead shark
uses its head to hold its prey against the
seafloor before eating it!

Tiger shark babies

sometimes eat one another
before they're born!

The cookiecutter shark

takes perfectly round
bites out of its prey.

The spotted wobbegong shark

has a beard that looks like seaweed. Unsuspecting prey
swim right up to its mouth and wind up inside.

The dwarf-lantern shark is the smallest shark,

measuring in at only six to eight inches
(15–20 cm) long or the length of an adult human hand.

DID YOU KNOW . . . ?

Sand dollars are not money.

Sea cucumbers are not cucumbers.

Let's get to know some fish who would DOLPHINITELY break your fishing pole!

May I point out that a DOLPHIN is actually an ocean mammal and NOT a fish?

The Whale Shark

This gentle giant of the sea clocks in at forty feet (12 m) in length and weighs anywhere from twenty-two thousand to forty-one thousand pounds (10,000–19,000 kg)! But perhaps its BIGGEST claim to fame is its massive five-foot-wide (1.5-meter-wide) mouth!

A small grownup could stand in that thing!

And while you might imagine that a shark with a mouth that big would stuff it full of all-you-can-eat seafood, the truth is, it typically only eats tiny plankton and small fish.

The Mekong Giant Catfish

The world's largest freshwater catfish won't fit on a plate or even a platter, but it would take up an entire dining room table. It comes in at up to ten feet (3 m) long and weighs up to 646 pounds (293 kg).

Some catfish have whiskers known as "barbels."

The Ocean Sunfish

The heavyweight champion of bony fish clocks in at a whopping five thousand pounds (2,300 kg)!

That fish weighs more than a minivan!

But it didn't start out that way. At birth, the ocean sunfish fry is no bigger than a tiny bug, but over its lifetime, the biggest ones will grow in size about sixty *million* times!

That's a big fish pancake!

The Megalodon

The megalodon lived 20 million to 2.6 million years ago and remains one of the largest predators that ever lived. This ancient shark could grow up to sixty feet (18 m) long and weigh nearly sixty tons (54,000 kg).

THE JELLY JOINT

GET SOME JELLY IN YOUR BELLY!
OPEN 24 HOURS

MENU

APPETEAZERS

JELLYFISH IN A BLANKET $4.99

IGNITE YOUR TASTE BUDS WITH THE STINGING SENSATION OF LIVE BOX
JELLYFISH SNUGGLED INSIDE WARM CRESCENT ROLLS. TENTACLES PACKED
WITH POISON-FILLED DARTS INCLUDED. THESE TASTE BABIES ARE LITERALLY
LETHAL! SIDE EFFECTS INCLUDE: INTENSE BACKACHE, HEADACHE, NAUSEA,
AND ANXIETY. NOT RECOMMENDED FOR EATING.

BONELESS BUFFALO JELLYFISH $6.99

NO BACKBONES HERE—YOU'RE IN INVERTEBRATE COUNTRY NOW, BABY! ENJOY
A WHOLE SMACK OF FIVE LIVE, BONELESS, GOLDEN JELLYFISH HAND-TOSSED IN
YOUR CHOICE OF HOT, MEDIUM, OR MILD DIPPING SAUCE! (CELERY AND BLUE
CHEESE $1 EXTRA.) THERE ARE OVER 25 TYPES OF EDIBLE JELLYFISH, BUT
YOU WON'T FIND ANY OF THEM HERE!

BLOOMIN' JELLYFISH $8.99

A WHOLE BLOOM—OR GROUP—OF BLOOMIN' JELLYFISH?! THAT'S WHAT
WE CALL "MORE THAN A MOUTHFUL"! HARVESTED FROM THE SAME SWARM,
THESE DEEP-FRIED BRAINLESS WONDERS WILL ASSAULT YOUR MOUTH WITH
FLAVOR! FLAVOR NOT INCLUDED. THESE JELLYFISH ARE ALIVE AND NOT
MEANT FOR HUMAN CONSUMPTION. GO EAT A SALAD OR SOMETHING.

CLASSIC BREAKFAST NACHOS WITH JELLYFISH $10.99

TORTILLA CHIPS, SHREDDED CHEESE, REFRIED JELLYFISH BEANS,
JALAPEÑOS, AND SOUR CREAM, TOPPED OFF WITH A 14-INCH (35 CM)
FRIED EGG JELLYFISH WHO DIDN'T ASK TO BE HERE! NO EGGS INCLUDED.
THIS IS JUST A JELLYFISH WE CAUGHT IN THE MEDITERRANEAN SEA WHO
HAPPENS TO LOOK LIKE A FRIED EGG FROM ABOVE. IF THESE NACHOS LOOK
GOOD TO YOU, YOU'LL ORDER THEM AND SET THIS INEDIBLE LITTLE GUY FREE!

DEZERT

JELLYFISH-FILLED DONUT $5.99

I DON'T THINK YOU'RE READY FOR THIS JELLY! TRY OUR TENDER DEEP-FRIED DONUT WITH THE HEART OF A JELLYFISH FILLING THE HOLE INSIDE. JELLYFISH DO NOT HAVE HEARTS. OR BRAINS. AND THEY DOLPHINITELY DO NOT BELONG IN A DONUT.

DRINKZ

JELLYFISH $1.00 (FREE REEF-ILLS!)

THESE LITTLE THIRST QUENCHERS ARE 95% WATER! *DO NOT DRINK THIS JELLYFISH! YOU ARE LIKE 60% WATER AND NO ONE IS THREATENING TO DRINK YOU!

*NOT FOR HUMANS TO EAT. SEA CREATURES ONLY!

KIDZ MENU

PEANUT BUTTER AND JELLYFISH SANDWICH $FREE.99

A GLOW-IN-YOUR-MOUTH SANDWICH?! OUR FAMOUS PB&J IS MADE UP OF A BIOLUMINESCENT COMB JELLYFISH, STUCK BETWEEN TWO SLICES OF STALE WHITE BREAD BY THE STICKIEST PEANUT BUTTER WE COULD SCRAPE OUT OF A JAR. WHY WOULD YOU EVEN THINK ABOUT ORDERING THIS? BIOLUMINESCENT JELLYFISH MAKE THEIR OWN LIGHT. THIS INTERNAL GLOW IS NATURE'S MAGIC AND DOES NOT BELONG IN YOUR LITTLE BELLY!

SEA CREATURE CONFESSIONAL

Female Lobster

"I PEE OUT OF MY EYEBALLS!"

In order to attract a male lobster, the female lobster will hover outside of his den and pee out of special nozzles located under her eyeballs. Her pee contains message-transmitting chemicals known as pheromones to let him know she's lookin' for love!

Argonaut Octopus

"I WILL GIVE YOU MY ARM IF YOU PROMISE NOT TO EAT ME!"

I LOVE YOU SO MUCH I COULD EAT YOU!

WHY ARE YOU SO AFRAID OF GETTING CLOSE TO ME?!

When it comes to mating, male octopuses have been known to be strangled and eaten by their larger female partners.

But some species of male octopus—like the argonaut octopus—have evolved to be able to remove their special "mating arm," hand it over to the female, and swim away like their life depends on it.

She then takes this arm, uses it to fertilize her eggs, and they both live happily ever after.

ACTUALLY, these octodads are semelparous animals, which means they reproduce once and then they die.

GASP!

Dumbo Octopus

"I FLAP MY EARS TO FLY!"

Despite its gigantic eyes, the world's deepest-living known octopus has a difficult time seeing along the ocean floor. But, little suckers on its tentacles serve as special sensors, allowing it to feel its way around the deep ocean waters. The dumbo octopus is also able to flap two large earlike fins to help it "fly" through the water!

Male Seahorse

"I'M A DAD! AND A MOM!"

I'M PREGNANT!

I'M YOUR MOM!

I'M YOUR DAD!

When male and female seahorses are ready to make baby seahorses, they'll join tails, dance through the water, and change colors. And while they're dancing, the female dumps her eggs into the male's pouch.

The male fertilizes the eggs, enjoys his breezy ten-to-twenty-five-day pregnancy, and POP! Out of the pouch come up to two thousand baby seahorses!

SUNKEN SHIP CRUISE LINES

Looking for some added WOW on your next underwater cruise? Please enjoy any of our exciting entertainment options!

Hagfish Presents HOW TO MAKE SLIME

Have you ever wondered how a disturbed hagfish can fill a one-gallon (3.8-L) bucket with mucus in a matter of minutes? Well, here's your chance to find out! Join our award-winning slime spinner as she reveals all of her slippery secrets!

Optical Illusions
SEEING DOUBLE

Set your sights on a four-eyed fish as he splits his vision in half horizontally! Marvel at his ability to swim with half of each eye out of the water, searching for insects, and half surveying the scene below! Two eyes, two retinas, four pupils, and a whole lot of WOW!

Feast Your Eyes
AN UNDERWATER GUIDE TO EATING EYEBALLS

Did you know that some fish eat the eyeballs of other fish? Join our artist-in-residence, Malawi eyebiter from Africa's Lake Malawi, for this one-of-a-kind, eye-popping experience!

Mucus Cocoon-Building Workshop

Learn how to build your own mucus cocoon from an experienced and skilled parrotfish! Parrotfish and wrasses use this mucus-cocoon-spinning technique to fend off moray eels and blood-sucking parasitic invertebrates at night. And soon, you can too! (Class size is limited.)

Decorate Yourself
HOW TO DESIGN ULTIMATE UNDERWATER CAMOUFLAGE

Does the thought of mingling make you want to crawl out of your shell? The decorator crab will help you blend into any under-the-sea situation. Work with seaweed, sponges, and coral to create the ultimate underwater camouflage.

Flying Lessons

Get ready to jump and glide with a giant trevally and a flying fish! Learn how to leap out of the water to catch birds in midair! Discover how a pair of winglike fins can help you glide above water to escape those annoying big fish down below. Who says fish can't fly?

DOLPHINITELY OR DOLPHINITELY NOT?

Dolphins are highly intelligent and social aquatic mammals. See if you can guess which of these facts about dolphins are dolphinitely TRUE or dolphinitely NOT!

1. The hippopotamus is the closest living relative to the dolphin.

DOLPHINITELY! Based on the fossil record, the dolphin's ancestor was a land mammal related to the hippo!

2. Some dolphins use jellyfish to protect their noses from sharp rocks and dangerous animals like sea urchins.

DOLPHINITELY NOT! Some dolphins use SEA SPONGES to protect their noses from deep-sea dangers.

3. Dolphins sleep with only half of their brain at a time.

DOLPHINITELY! When a dolphin sleeps, only half its brain goes to sleep. The other half stays active, allowing for the dolphin to come up to the water's surface to breathe.

4. A bottlenose dolphin using echolocation makes sixty clicking sounds per minute.

DOLPHINITELY NOT! A bottlenose dolphin using echolocation makes ONE THOUSAND clicking sounds per SECOND!

5. Most dolphins have a melon between their eyes.

DOLPHINITELY! The "melon" is a special sensory organ located between the eyes of most dolphins. They use it to help them gather and focus sound waves.

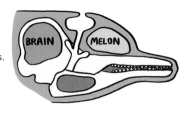

BRAIN   MELON

NO POOP

6. Dolphins poop out of their blowholes.

DOLPHINITELY NOT! Silly human! Dolphins use their blowholes to BREATHE!

Fact Snacks

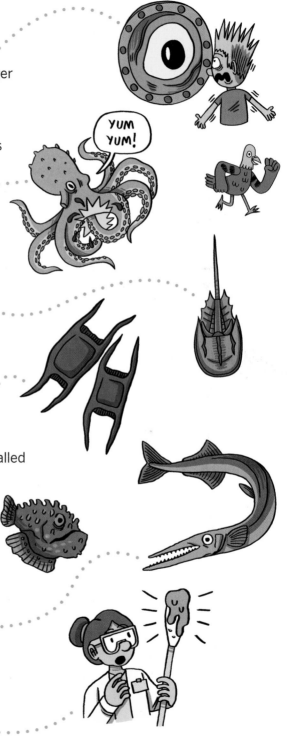

★ One eyeball of a giant squid is bigger than a whole human head!

★ The giant octopus sometimes eats its own arms!

★ Horseshoe crabs are related to spiders, not crabs, and have looked the same for at least three hundred million years!

★ The manta ray has a fin span that's about the same width as a small plane's wingspan, twenty-two feet (6.7 m) wide.

★ Skate egg cases are sometimes called "mermaid's purses."

★ Stonefish, the most venomous fish in the sea, look like ordinary rocks on the seafloor.

★ The garfish has green bones!

★ Scientists can estimate how old a whale is by examining its earwax.

WILD THINGS
TONGUE TWISTERS

Anteater

With a super-sticky tongue that can grow up to two feet (61 cm) long, the giant anteater is able to lap up almost thirty thousand ants and termites in a single day! Here's how: The anteater identifies a good picnic spot—either a termite or ant mound—breaks it open, and rapidly flicks its tongue into the tunnels up to 150 times a minute! Once its tongue is covered in tiny insects, it zings them into its mouth, and will likely come back for seconds!

Hummingbird

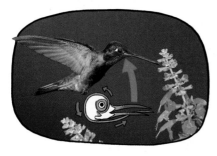

The hummingbird's tongue is so long, it can measure up to *twice* the length of its beak. In fact, when retracted back inside its beak, its tongue can wrap up inside its head, coiling around its brain and eyeballs! But it's what this tongue does outside the body that really WOWS. The hummingbird uses its tongue to reach deep into flowers, pumping out the nectar at a practically lightning-fast speed.

150

Chameleon

The chameleon's mouth is home to the quickest tongue *in the world!* Just how quick is it? Well, if a chameleon's tongue was a car, it would be able to accelerate to sixty miles per hour (97 kph) in just ten milliseconds. The chameleon uses its tongue almost like a sticky lasso when targeting its prey. When it's ready to strike, the chameleon contracts its tongue muscles. Then, using its excellent eyesight, it lines up its target and releases. This launches its tongue out of its mouth at an incredible speed and with incredible power.

Giraffe

The giraffe's tongue comes in at a whopping twelve to twenty-one inches (30–53 cm) long! It's also one of the toughest tongues in the world, being made out of a very thick, leatherlike substance.

So what does a giraffe do with a tongue like this? Well, just like you, it eats! But, a giraffe's favorite food is LEAVES! Specifically, leaves from super thorny trees found in Africa. Having a long tongue helps it prod around to find the leaves, while the tongue's thickness protects it from getting pricked.

Blue Whale

It might come as no surprise that the largest animal in the world also has the heaviest tongue in the world. The tongue of a blue whale weighs in at a whopping wow of 2.7 tons (2,500 kg). That's almost as heavy as two midsize cars!

CREEPY CRAWLERS

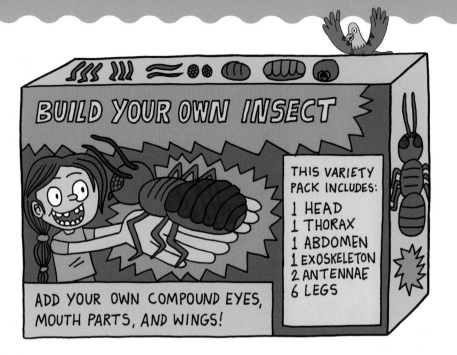

BUILD YOUR OWN INSECT

THIS VARIETY PACK INCLUDES:

1 HEAD
1 THORAX
1 ABDOMEN
1 EXOSKELETON
2 ANTENNAE
6 LEGS

ADD YOUR OWN COMPOUND EYES, MOUTH PARTS, AND WINGS!

BUG GRUB

WHEN IT COMES TO EATING, YOU'VE TRIED IT ALL . . .

OH, I'M A CARNIVORE, I ONLY EAT MEAT.

OH, I RECENTLY BECAME AN HERBIVORE. I ONLY EAT PLANTS.

I'M AN OMNIVORE NOW! NOW I EAT PLANTS AND MEAT!

SO WHY NOT TRY THE EATING CRAZE THAT MOST BIRDS AND SOME REPTILES ARE RAVING ABOUT!

BECOME AN INSECTIVORE TODAY!

WHAT'S AN INSECTIVORE?

AN INSECTIVORE IS AN ANIMAL OR PLANT THAT GETS MOST OF ITS NUTRIENTS FROM EATING INSECTS!

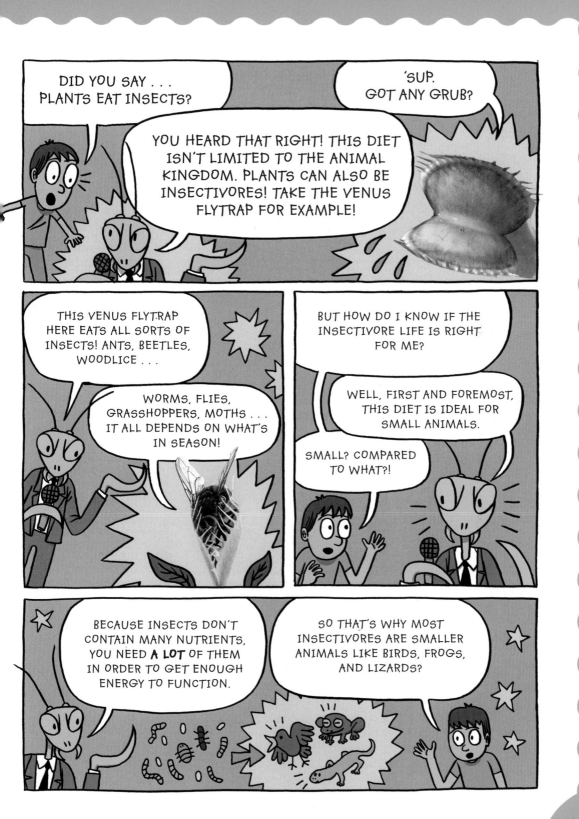

DIRTY JOBS: THE INSECT EDITION

When it comes to the animal kingdom, every creature has a job to do. These jobs not only help to support an animal's family and community, but they also help to provide the animal with basic necessities like food and shelter. Here are some of the dirtiest jobs we found in the insect world!

Dung Beetle

"WE'RE THE POOP-EATING PROS!"

Licensed to work on every continent except for Antarctica! Here's how we get the job done:

"I'm a roller. This means I create big balls of poop from even bigger piles of animal droppings, and then I ROLL them away from the pile. Then I bury the balls partially underground for safekeeping. I do this so I can come back later to chow down or even just lay my eggs."

In relation to its body size, the dung beetle is not only one of the strongest insects in the world, it's one of the strongest ANIMALS in the world. The roller can push 1,141 times its own body weight! That's like a human being pushing six fully loaded double-decker buses down the street!

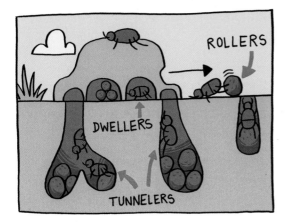

"We're tunnelers. As tunnelers, my partner and I dive headfirst into a stinkin' pile of dung. I organize the space while he goes up and collects the poop. He then brings it back to me so I can start the chow down!"

How thoughtful!

IT'S NOT CHOCOLATE, IT'S POOP!

"I'm what they call a dweller. And as you probably guessed, if I see a big ol' pile of poop, I'm gonna LIVE on top of it! We dwellers set up shop right on top, and when we're ready to reproduce, we'll lay our eggs there in the poop! This way, when our eggs hatch, our dung beetle babies are surrounded by poop to eat so they can grow into big and strong dung beetle adults. Like me!"

Dermestids

"CALL US FOR ALL OF YOUR FLESH-CLEANING NEEDS!"

Using a special process called skeletonization, we will feast on the flesh of any dead animal carcass, so you don't have to!

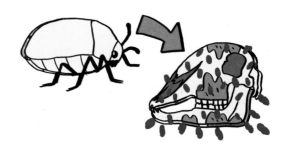

★ As one of the most essential workers in the wild, we're here to help with all of your decomposition needs. That's how *we* guarantee *you* a healthy ecosystem!

★ With us, NO flesh goes uneaten, and NO bones are harmed, or your money back!

Jewel Wasp

"WE TURN COCKROACHES INTO ZOMBIES!"

Tired of creeping cockroaches? Then call us! As masters of mind control, we use a four-pronged plan of attack to get those roaches out of your life once and for all. How? By turning them into zombies for our personal use! Let's take a look at this roach-buster in action:

Step 1: The elegant jewel wasp injects the cockroach's brain with her powerful venom, which turns him into a zombified version of his former self.

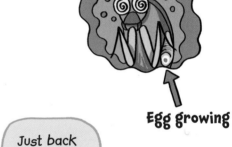

Step 2: She lures the zombie roach into her burrow.

Step 3: She lays her eggs on the roach's leg.

Step 4: The zombie roach lives out his final days as food for her larvae.

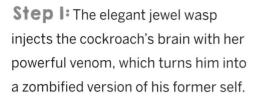

Egg growing

Ewwww.

Just back away slowly.

HOME CREEP HOME

Even creepy-crawlies need a place to crawl home! Insect homes come in all shapes and sizes, each serving its own unique purpose. Whether you prefer communal living or a party of one, when you're an insect, there's no place like home.

Spittlebug's House of Bubbles

Contrary to popular belief, my home is NOT made out of spit. It's made out of pee. I formed my home using a mix of my own urine and a sticky fluid I make in my abdomen. This combo helped to create the air-filled bubbles that I call home!

Should be called a PIDDLEbug!

Termite Towers

We termites are famous for designing some of the most impressive structures in the insect world. With 550 pounds (250 kg) of dirt, a few tons of water, and some serious teamwork, we can build a mound up to seventeen feet (5 m) tall. And that's not all! As tiny termites, we know how vulnerable we are to sunlight.

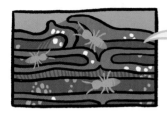

That's why we design our mounds to help ensure that we never see the light of day. Each one comes with its own built-IN vertical farm and fungal food garden. Farming! Food! Function! Fantastic! Let us design your termite tower today!

Welcome to the Beehive

HOME OF HONEYCOMB HEXAGON DESIGN

Come see what all the buzz is about! Our beehives are not only one of the most iconic homes in the insect world, but they also boast some serious storage! Whether it's eggs from the queen, pollen from the meadow, or that sweet, sweet honey we can't get enough of, our unique honeycomb hexagon storage system can house it all! Come see why over a million bees agree that the interlocking hexagon design is the strongest and most efficient way to store our stuff. Similar shapes like circles would leave gaps that would need to be filled with our hard-earned wax. And we don't waste wax! In fact, the honeycomb hexagonal structure is so efficient that humans have used this design in their own architecture. See if you can spot it strengthening buildings and bridges.

NO WASTED WAXES!

Who knew humans were such wanna-bees?!

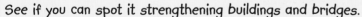

PACK OF PESTS

Hercules Beetle

The Hercules beetle, a type of rhinoceros beetle, is one of the strongest beetles on earth for its size. How strong is it? The Hercules beetle can carry 850 times its own weight!

That's like me carrying seven elephants!

Giant Long-Legged Katydid

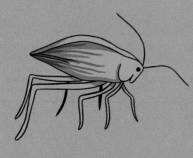

This long-legged, leafy-looking master of disguise hides all day and hops all night. Its natural ability to blend in with plants and trees helps to protect it from predators. And by the way, did we mention that some katydids can grow to be bigger than a human hand?

Assassin Bug

With a straw for a mouth, the assassin bug injects its prey with a toxin so powerful, it LIQUEFIES THE PREY'S INSIDES! It then uses this same straw-like mouth to suck up all the guts.

Girl's gotta eat!

Giant Burrowing Cockroach

Weighing in at almost as much as a golf ball, the giant burrowing cockroach, also known as the rhinoceros cockroach, is the heaviest cockroach species in the world! You can find it burrowing 3.3 feet (1 m) deep beneath the ground in Australia.

Titan Beetle

At 6.5 inches (16.5 cm) long, the titan beetle is the largest known beetle in the Amazon rainforest, and sports a set of mandibles (jaws) strong enough to snap a pencil in half!

Thorn Bug

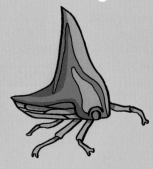

This over-the-top treehopper features a massive thorn on its head resembling a spiky, full-body hat! Hungry birds scouring the fruit trees of south Florida don't even know it's there, because it disguises itself to look like a thorn on a branch. Sneaky little thorn bug!

BAD HABITS:
THE BUG EDITION

Housefly

I . . . eat my own vomit. You see, I don't have a mouth to bite or chew food. So when I'm hungry, I have to use my FEET to taste food. If I like the taste, I'll barf on the food since my vomit contains the digestive enzymes to break down the food. At this point, I can use my spongelike tongue to soak up the barfy food to get nutrients I need. Is that bad?

No, that's perfectly natural! I do it all the time.

Really?

No.

Exploding Ant

Hi, I am a COLOBOPSIS EXPLODENS, but you can just call me Exploding Ant. Let's see, where do I begin? I'm, uh . . . extremely loyal, and I will stop at nothing to protect my colony, even if that means I have to explode my guts all over an intruder.

Tell us what you mean by EXPLODE.

Well, if a predator attempts to attack me or my colony, I will literally explode.

Explode what?

My whole body! Guts everywhere. Which coats my predator in a poisonous yellow goo. And it's all to protect my family. I can't help it!

Maybe we need to work on your temper?

Honeybee Queen

I am famous for my quacks and toots!

Did you say . . . quacking? Tooting?

Allow me to explain. When I'm ready to bust out of the honeycomb cell where I grew up and make my grand entrance, I'll start quacking to alert my colony that A QUEEN IS READY TO LEAD!

So, sort of like a bugle call?

Exactly. Bees! Prepare for your royal highness!

And the tooting?

Well, I'll move around the colony, tooting up a storm in order to announce my presence.

That's one way to do it.

My tooting also serves as a strong signal to my worker bees that they better seal up any other queens and hold them captive so I can reign supreme until I'm ready to move on!

But what if another queen emerges before your workers have a chance to stop her?

THERE CAN ONLY BE ONE QUEEN!

Sorry I asked!

I will fight her to her death.

Yikes!

There can only be ONE QUEEN. Bwahahahahaha!

Thanks for chatting with us!

Caterpillar

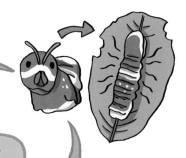

I have a habit of making myself look like poop.

Uh . . . poop?

Yeah! See, someday I'll transform into a beautiful black-and-yellow Asian swallowtail butterfly, but for now, I just look like a pile of bird poop.

It's my spine, see? It's black and white, just like bird poop. So when a bird comes around looking for a snack, they're going to skip right over me because I just look like a big pile of their own . . .

Poop. Yeah, we got it.

Don't worry, it's literally just a growth stage, and thanks to your poopy looks, you'll get to grow out of it!

Cockroach

I do this weird thing where, after I've had my head cut off, I continue to run around like everything is normal.

Uhh.

Yeah, so I don't actually need my head to breathe. My brain doesn't even control my breathing. I get oxygen through these little holes in my body segments called SPIRACLES, and they help deliver the oxygen to the rest of my body.

But your head! It's detached!

Thanks, I noticed. See, the only thing I really need my head for is eating, and I can go for at least a week without food, so . . .

Uhh.

So you can run around decapitated for a week or until you get hungry? That's BONKERBALLS!

Ladybug

When I get scared, I squirt stinky juice from my knees.

What?!

Yeah, I'm so quirky!

But . . . why?

PREDATORS. When I'm frightened by a predator, I will activate my knees and let out an odor so foul it will blow them away.

Can you describe the smell? I'm interested in getting some for my knees.

Oh, sure! It's basically a disgusting combo of nuts, green bell peppers, potatoes, and mold. Predators don't stand a chance against my signature stink!

HIGH-FIVE!

EIGHT WAYS THAT SPIDERS WOW!

Spiders are EVERYWHERE! More than forty-five thousand species of these eight-legged arachnids can be found all over the world!

THE FEMALE BLACK WIDOW SPIDER'S VENOM IS FIFTEEN TIMES STRONGER THAN THE VENOM OF A RATTLESNAKE.

MUCH LIKE HOW A PORCUPINE HAS SHARP QUILLS TO DEFEND ITSELF, NEW-WORLD TARANTULAS HAVE TINY, IRRITATING HAIRS THAT THEY FLING AT POTENTIAL PREDATORS TO KEEP THEM AT BAY.

A FISHING SPIDER CAN STAY UNDERWATER FOR THIRTY MINUTES WHILE WAITING TO CATCH ITS PREY.

ANTS CAN BE SPIDERS IN DISGUISE! ANT-MIMICKING SPIDERS PRETEND TO BE ANTS BY RAISING TWO OF THEIR EIGHT LEGS TO LOOK LIKE ANT ANTENNAE.

All spiders on earth combined weigh about twenty-five million tons (22,700,000 t).

And they come in a variety of shapes and sizes, too! From the 0.011-inch (0.28-cm) tiny Samoan moss spider to the nearly foot-long (30-cm) leg span of the goliath birdeater tarantula, spiders are packed with WOW!

SAMOAN MOSS SPIDER →

GOLIATH BIRDEATER TARANTULA

THE BOLAS SPIDER USES A LONG STRAND OF SILK LIKE A STICKY-ENDED FISHING LINE BY SWINGING IT AT NEARBY MOTHS TO CATCH AND REEL THEM IN.

THE FEMALE TRASHLINE ORB WEAVER HOARDS POOP AND TRASH IN HER WEB, THEN HIDES HERSELF AND HER EGG CASES INSIDE OF THE WASTE.

FOR ITS WEIGHT, SPIDERWEB SILK IS TOUGHER AND STRONGER THAN STEEL.

THE MALE BLACK WIDOW SPIDER WILL FORCE-FEED HIMSELF TO THE FEMALE BY PLACING HIMSELF IN HER MANDIBLES UNTIL SHE EVENTUALLY DECIDES TO EAT HIM.

BLACK WIDOW

Fact Snacks

★ Mosquitoes love your stinky feet! There is a specific bacteria that grows on human feet, and mosquitoes have trouble resisting it.

★ Housefly feet are ten million times more sensitive than the human tongue. They use their feet to locate sugar.

yummy!

SUGAR

★ The water scorpion uses its tail as a snorkel to breathe underwater.

★ Bulldog ants can leap seven times the length of their bodies.

★ The ant-eating assassin bug confuses its predators by piling its victims onto its body in a massive ball.

★ Dragonflies have existed on earth for more than three hundred million years. They were some of the first winged insects to ever evolve.

* Fruit flies were the first living creatures intentionally launched into space.

* Grasshoppers roamed the earth before dinosaurs ever even existed.

* The diamondback ironclad beetle has an exoskeleton so hard, it can survive being run over by a car.

* Ladybugs are not actually bugs at all! They're beetles.

I DON'T LIKE LABELS!

* The trap-jaw ant can swim ten times faster than Olympic champion Michael Phelps.

* There are an estimated 10 QUINTILLION (10,000,000,000,000,000,000) individual insects alive.

TREND ALERT: EXOSKELETONS

STYLE INSPIDER

Here at *Style InSpider*, we believe that it's what's on the inside that really counts. But we also believe that if you've got it, FLAUNT IT! So stop hiding that beautiful skeleton of yours on the inside, and start showing it off for all the world to see.

Check out the biological adaptation that bugs—and crustaceans!—can't stop buzzing about!

Most invertebrates have an exoskeleton of some sort, and all arthropods have one.

A whopping 98 percent of all known animals don't have backbones, and around 96 percent don't have bones at all! So where do they turn to for support? Sometimes, the answer is: EXOSKELETONS!

The arthroPOD
Insects
Millipedes and centipedes
Spiders and scorpions
Prawns and crabs,
as well as
other crustaceans!

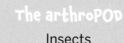

I wear my exoskeleton like a suit of armor. It even has flexible joints to help me wiggle around!

I wear my exoskeleton to help hide my soft, vulnerable side.

I wear my skeleton on the inside to keep people from freaking out!

Help! I'm busting out of my exoskeleton!

Exoskeleton getting a little too tight? Well, good news! Outgrowing your old exoskeleton is a perfectly natural part of arthropod life!

RIIIIP!

12 px

Experts recommend shedding your old uncomfortable husk in a process known as ecdysis, or molting.

Out with the old and in with the new! Once you start molting, you'll be free to form a brand-new exoskeleton with a much roomier fit!

HUSKS & STUFF
★ CASH! CASH!

WE WANT THE STUFF YOU DON'T!

SKINS!

"WHEN IT WAS TIME FOR ME TO GROW OUT OF MY OLD SKIN, HUSKS & STUFF WAS RIGHT THERE, READY TO PAY ME TOP DOLLAR!"

HUSKS!

"SURE, MY EXOSKELETON FIT WHILE I WAS A WEE NYMPH DEVELOPING UNDERGROUND, BUT ONCE I GREW INTO A FULL-SIZE CICADA, IT WAS TIME TO BREAK FREE FROM THAT OLD HUSK, GIVING MY NEW WINGS A CHANCE TO FLY! HUSKS & STUFF BOUGHT MY OLD HUSK, NO QUESTIONS ASKED!"

WE PAY MORE!

SHELLS!

"ANYONE WHO KNOWS ME KNOWS THAT MY SHELL IS MY MOBILE HOME. WITHOUT IT, I WOULD ROAST IN THE HOT TROPICAL SUN! THAT'S WHY, WHEN I'M READY TO UPGRADE TO A LARGER SHELL TO CALL HOME, I ALWAYS BUY AND SELL AT HUSKS & STUFF!"

WE'LL BUY JUST ABOUT ANYTHING!

WE'VE GOT A VARIETY OF QUALITY SHELLS IN ALL SIZES! COME SEE US WHEN YOU'RE LOOKING FOR YOUR NEXT CRUSTACEAN KINGDOM!

WILD THINGS

SMELL YA LATER! WORLD'S MOST STINKTASTIC ANIMALS

I thought that smell was coming from you, Mindy!

SKUNK

Not this time, Guy Raz . . . LOOK!

When frightened or threatened by a predator, the western spotted skunk zeros in on its target by performing a handstand, while keeping its eyes on the attacker as it lines up its butt and lets it RIP! A smelly and oily substance sprays from a gland underneath the skunk's tail and can shoot at a distance of up to fifteen feet (4.6 m)! And although the spray isn't harmful, the foul smell can last for days.

WHAT IN THE WOW?

A group of skunks is called a surfeit, and a baby skunk is called a kit.

STINK BUG

I WOULDN'T EAT ME IF I WERE YOU! *TOOT!*

Much like the skunk, the stink bug usually only releases its super-stink powers when under attack from a predator. And once that musky, odorous liquid is let loose, it can haunt a room for hours! If it comes in contact with

your skin, it could take several scrubs to get the stench out. The stink bug uses its power of extreme odor to discourage other animals from eating it.

WOW TIP

If you spot a stink bug in your house, don't reach for your slipper or rolled-up newspaper. The worst smell the stink bug emits happens when it's *crushed*. In that case, the odor is likely to stick around for days!

BINTURONG

The binturong, also known as the bearcat, can be found in the treetops of jungles in Southeast Asia. It has the soft, pudgy body of a bear, the face of a cat, and pee that smells like hot buttered popcorn.

What?! Here's how it works: the binturong soaks its feet and tail in its own pee, then smears its pee-soaked tail over tree branches and trunks to mark its territory.

But why does it smell like hot buttered popcorn?? Well, it all has to do with a chemical compound called 2-AP. This chemical is found all through the binturong's pee and just so happens to be the same chemical compound that gives popcorn its yummy smell!

STINKBIRD

Do you *see* what I smell?

In the Amazon and Orinoco Delta in South America, there lives a bird with a serious stench. The hoatzin, aka the stinkbird, belches a type of methane known for its pungent, manure-like aroma.

AH! It's attacking my olfactory senses!

AWESOME AMPHIBIANS

ARE YOU AN AMPHIBIAN?

1. My dream home is somewhere . . .

- **(A)** Crazy cold with icebergs
- **(B)** Always cold and always wet
- **(C)** Warm and tropical
- **(D)** Hot and dry with no water

2. Do others call you "spineless"?

- **(A)** Yes, all the time!
- **(B)** No, my spine is literally the backbone of my whole body.

3. Does your internal body temperature change with your surroundings?

- **(A)** Yes, it's out of control!
- **(B)** No, I am in complete control of regulating and maintaining my own body temperature, thank you very much!

4. How were you born?

- **(A)** I popped out of my birth mom!
- **(B)** I sprouted from a seed!
- **(C)** MAGIC!
- **(D)** I busted out of an egg!

5. Your skin is best described as . . .

- **(A)** Super slimy
- **(B)** Slippery
- **(C)** Scaly
- **(D)** All of the above except for C

6. Your skin can do cool tricks like . . .

- **(A)** Breathe and absorb water
- **(B)** Change colors to match your moods
- **(C)** Fall off
- **(D)** Stick to anything

7. When you were a baby you . . .

(A) Lived underwater
(B) Had no legs
(C) Used gills to breathe
(D) Were so cute, you made people barf
(E) All of the above

8. Now that you're grown, you can . . .

(A) Spend most of your time on land
(B) Spend most of your time in the water
(C) Breathe with the help of your cute new lungs
(D) Any of the above

If your answers match most or all of the correct answers, CONGRATULATIONS! YOU ARE AN AMPHIBIAN! So why are you even reading this book? You're probably getting it all wet and gross! Put this book down and go play in the water or something.

For the rest of you, here's what you should know about amphibians. Amphibians are slimy vertebrates (that means they have backbones) that need water or a wet environment to survive and thrive. They're cold blooded, which means they have trouble controlling their body temperature the way we humans do. Amphibians also have special skin that allows them to absorb water, oxygen, and carbon dioxide.

Most amphibians will go through extreme transformations in their lifetimes. These transformations are known as metamorphosis. Through metamorphosis, an amphibian will transform from an egg to a larva (hi, tadpoles!) to an adult with four legs. Salamanders, newts, frogs, and toads are all amphibians, and *none of them can read this book.*

Eggs

DIARY OF A FROG:
A Journey through Metamorphosis

DAY 1: Hey guys, it's me. I'm an egg. Or at least, I'm INSIDE of an egg. Just one of the THOUSANDS that were laid here by my mother. My father stopped by to fertilize us, and then he was all, "You're on your own now! Peace out!" So, now I guess I'm just left here to develop alongside all these other spawn.

IT'S ME!

DAY 6: Well, some pretty big changes have occurred since you last heard from me. First of all, I now have gills. I guess now I should be able to breathe underwater? Oh, and I also grew a TAIL. That was . . . unexpected. Wait until you see what I'm talking about.

DAY 14: TA-DA! It was starting to get a little crammed in my egg casing, so I decided it was time to come out and greet the world! Hello, world! It is I, a wee little tadpole. And ugh. Busting out of this egg and away from the rest of the spawn really zapped my energy! I've just been eating what's left of this egg's yolk and chilling.

WEEK 4: I FINALLY put my gills and tail to good use and went for my first swim. It . . . was . . . AMAZING! I also found a bunch of new food to eat. So many delicious underwater plants around here. Guess I'm an herbivore now. Have you ever tried algae? It's the best!

YUM!

WEEK 6: WHOA. Get this—I have lungs now. I don't even know where they came from. One minute I'm breathing through my gills, and the next I'm filtering oxygen through my lungs?! Thinking I might try some yoga breathing exercises.

WEEK 8: Well, this week comes with some bittersweet news. My tail is starting to . . . disappear. (There, I said it.) At this point, I don't know whether or not I'll ever lose it completely, but I can tell you that weird legs are growing in its place. Oh, and each leg has a WEBBED foot at the end. What am I supposed to do with webbed feet?!

WEEK 9: My tail is getting shorter, my back legs are getting longer, the webbed feet are still kickin', and—get this—I now have FRONT LEGS too! Apparently they're called "forelimbs"? I will say, they do make getting around A LOT easier.

WOW!

WEEK 13: Major changes over here. Like, if I had a mirror, I wouldn't even recognize myself. My little stump of a tail is just about gone completely. I'm also happy to announce that I have become a WAY more adventurous eater; I eat insects now! Also, skin has grown over my gills and I can venture OUTSIDE the water now. I mean, not too far. I will always consider myself "semiaquatic," but still! I plan to spend half my time inside the water, and half of my time outside of it. Oh, and this means I can now hop on land! Anyone with legs should try it. Highly recommended.

PS. This just in: My metamorphosis is complete. I am no longer a tadpole, I AM A PROUD FROG.

FROG

2 YEARS LATER: Just checking in to say that life has been good. Some would say I've "found my voice" and spend a lot of time croaking kroakaoke. It's fun. But not as fun as hiding from unsuspecting insects, shooting my long sticky tongue at them, and snapping them up to eat. HAHA I'm SO BAD!!

4 YEARS LATER: BIG NEWS! I just laid my first four thousand eggs. Meet my spawn. Aren't they beautiful?

THE AMPHIBIAN AWARDS

And the award goes to . . .

Poison Dart Frog
MOST LIKELY TO KILL

The poison dart frog is one of the most recognizable frogs on the planet. With striking bright colors, it stands out in the tropical forests of South America. It's also known as the most toxic animal on the planet! So toxic, in fact, that the Emberá people of Colombia have traditionally used the poison dart frog to make deadly weapons. They'd dip the tips of their darts in the poison glands of the frog. When used, these poison darts would paralyze their target.

So *that's* how the poison dart frog got its name!

Actually, I heard it was a family name.

189

Olm Salamander
MOST LIKELY TO NEVER LEAVE TOWN

When it comes to the Lazy Olympics, the olm salamander is the one to beat. It's colorless, almost blind, can live for up to one hundred years, and can go years without moving or eating. In fact, it's *so* lazy that it preys on small insects by sitting very still with its mouth open, waiting for the food to walk in.

Emerald Glass Frog
MOST LIKELY TO BE CONFUSED FOR A GHOST

Deep in the rainforests of Central and South America, a tiny frog, only slightly larger than a quarter, bares its guts for all the world to see. That's because the glass frog's belly and legs are covered in see-through skin. In fact, this skin is so translucent that if you looked at the frog from underneath, you'd be able to see all its internal organs working to keep it alive, including its intestines and beating heart.

Surinam Toad
MOST LIKELY TO BE MISTAKEN FOR ROADKILL

With its wide, flat body and beady, lidless eyes sitting atop a tiny, flat, triangular head, the Surinam toad could be easily mistaken for dead. Unless you found her giving birth. Unlike any other animal on the planet, she holds her fertilized eggs in tiny holes formed on the skin of her back. When she's ready to give birth . . . POP! The fully formed babies burst from these holes, ready to make their way into the world. Look for them in the rainforest pools of Trinidad and Tobago and around the Amazon basin. Or DON'T!

FROG VS. TOAD

We've all been there. You're invited to an amphibian dinner party, and you mistakenly identify a frog as a toad, or vice versa! Your face turns red, your palms begin to sweat, and you vow to never misidentify the two again. To help you avoid this social snafu in the future, we've created a little primer to help you better understand the differences between these two similar-looking, yet surprisingly different, genetic cousins.

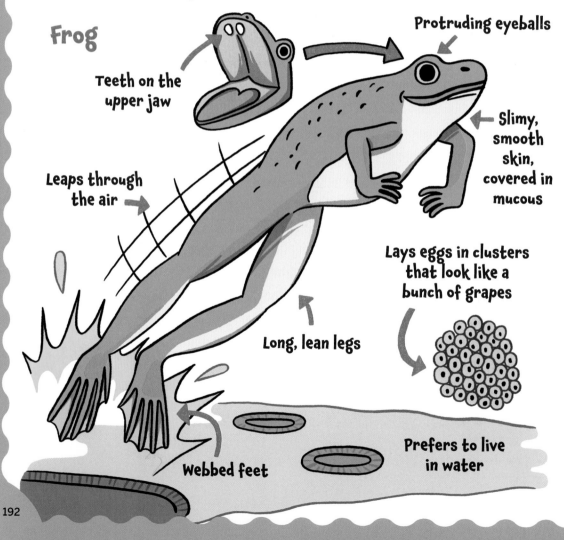

Frog

Teeth on the upper jaw

Protruding eyeballs

Slimy, smooth skin, covered in mucous

Leaps through the air

Lays eggs in clusters that look like a bunch of grapes

Long, lean legs

Webbed feet

Prefers to live in water

But of course, there are exceptions to the rule. While these guidelines do apply to most species, there are some frogs that have short and stubby legs, and some toads that have smooth and slimy skin. So if you get it wrong in the wild, don't be too hard on yourself. Just learn from your mistake and hop along.

Toad

Lays eggs in long strands, like a string of pearls

SHOW-OFF

Some have poisonous glands behind their eyes

Dry, rough skin, covered in warty-looking bumps

Stubby body

Toothless

Crawls on the ground, hops occasionally

Short legs

Prefers to live on dry land, near water

BIG AND SMALL

Goliath Frog

The goliath frog of West Africa can grow up to 12.5 inches (32 cm) long and weigh up to 7.2 pounds (3.3 kg). That's about the size and weight of a house cat! It should come as no surprise that the goliath frog is the largest frog in the world.

CROAK.

WORLD'S BIGGEST FROG

#1

But it didn't start out that way! Goliath frog tadpoles are no larger than other tadpoles!

But when they grow up, they just keep growing and growing and GROWING!

WHAT IN THE WOW?

Goliath frogs love to wrestle! When it comes time for mating season, the male frogs will make a large collection of rocks and gravel on the riverbank to attract females and then wrestle other male frogs for the right to breed with the females.

Paedophryne amauensis

The *Paedophryne amauensis* is not only the smallest frog in the animal kingdom, it's also arguably the smallest vertebrate. This tiny amphibian measures in at less than 0.3 inches (7.7 mm) and weighs as much as a housefly! It is found in the leaf litter covering the forest floors of Papua New Guinea, where it feasts on a diet of mites.

WORLD'S TINIEST FROG!

Not so fast!

Huh?

In 2019, three NEW species of frog were discovered in Madagascar!

Well, how small are they?

Ranging from eight to fifteen millimeters long, MINI MUM, MINI SCULE, and MINI ATURE are all small enough to fit on a thumbnail! (*Thumbs-up!*)

RIBBIT...

RIBBIT...

RIBBIT!

Mini mum

Mini scule

Mini ature

SALAMANDERS ARE STRANGE

Fact Snacks

I'VE GOT MY EYES ON YOU!

★ The four-eyed frog confuses predators with a butt boasting fake eyes.

★ The wood frog is the only frog that lives north of the Arctic Circle. It freezes solid in the winter and thaws in the spring. When frozen, its breathing, blood flow, and heartbeat completely stop, while its body creates an antifreeze-type substance that helps it to survive being a frozen frogsicle.

★ Wallace's flying frog can glide up to fifty feet (15.2 m) through the air, as it soars from tree to tree. It does this by spreading its large webbed toes, which act like sails to help it glide!

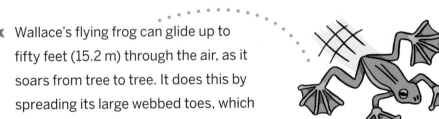

★ Male spring peeper frogs get together at the beginning of every spring to puff out their throat sacs and whistle loudly in an attempt to attract females.

★ If some newts lose or damage a leg, they can just grow a new one!

OUCH!

★ The word *amphibian* comes from "amphibios," which means "both lives" in Greek, because most amphibians begin their lives in water and eventually move to dry land.

WILD THINGS

MOBILE HOMES

ARE YOU TIRED OF BEING STUCK IN ONE PLACE YEAR AFTER YEAR?

UH . . . NO.

WOULD YOU DESCRIBE YOUR NATURAL HABITAT AS THE OPEN ROAD?

UM . . . NOT REALLY.

THEN MAYBE YOU SHOULD EXPERIENCE THE MOBILE LIFE!

HUH?

COME ON DOWN TO NOMADIC ANIMALS MOBILE HOME DEALERSHIP AND MAKE ALL OF YOUR TRAVELING DREAMS COME TRUE!

BUT I DON'T HAVE . . .

THIS COULD BE THE LIFE CHANGE YOU'VE BEEN LOOKING FOR. BUT DON'T TAKE MY WORD FOR IT. JUST LISTEN TO THESE SATISFIED CUSTOMERS.

NOMADIC ANIMALS MOBILE HOME DEALERSHIP

WHAT I LOVE MOST ABOUT MY MOBILE SHELL HOME IS THE SENSE OF SECURITY IT GIVES ME WHEN A PREDATOR IS NEARBY. I JUST PULL MY HEAD AND LIMBS INSIDE, AND LET THE HARDENED KERATIN DO THE TALKING!

TURTLE

THE ENTIRE SHELL IS MADE OF TWO PIECES. THE CARAPACE IS THE PIECE THAT FITS ATOP THE TURTLE'S BACK, AND THE PLASTRON IS THE PIECE THAT FITS UNDER ITS BELLY. BOTH SHELLS ARE COVERED WITH A THICK LAYER OF KERATIN—THE SAME STUFF THAT MAKES UP HUMAN FINGERNAILS!

THE TWO SEPARATE PIECES GIVE MY MOBILE SHELL HOME THE FLEXIBILITY FOR ME TO HIDE UNTIL DANGER PASSES.

MY FELLOW SNAIL SPECIES AND I ARE ALWAYS LOOKING FOR THE LATEST AND GREATEST IN MOBILE LIVING. AND BECAUSE WE LIVE IN HABITATS ALL OVER THE WORLD, WE HAVE TO DEAL WITH A LOT OF DIFFERENT ENVIRONMENTS. THE SHELLS WE CHOOSE NOT ONLY HELP PROTECT US FROM PREDATORS, BUT ALSO PROVIDE SHELTER FROM HARSH WEATHER CONDITIONS. FIVE STARS!

SNAIL

IF THE TEMPERATURE DROPS BELOW FREEZING, YOU'RE GOING TO WANT A PLACE TO CRAWL INTO, SEAL OFF WITH MUCUS, AND HIBERNATE UNTIL THINGS START TO HEAT UP AGAIN.

ALSO, I'M NOCTURNAL, SO SOMETIMES I LIKE TO CRAWL INSIDE JUST TO AVOID THE SUN.

AND BE SURE TO CHECK OUT OUR LATEST XL-SIZE MODEL, FIT FOR A GIANT AFRICAN SNAIL! THIS MASSIVE MOBILE HOME CAN GROW UP TO EIGHT INCHES (20 CM) IN LENGTH AND UP TO FOUR INCHES (10 CM) IN HEIGHT! TALK ABOUT A MOBILE MANSION!

AS A CRUSTACEAN WHO HAS BEEN CLIMBING UP THE PROPERTY LADDER SINCE I WAS JUST A WEE ZOEA, I'VE SPENT MY LIFE MOVING INTO NEW ABANDONED SHELLS EVERY TWELVE TO EIGHTEEN MONTHS. BUT AFTER YEARS OF FLIPPING SHELLS, I FINALLY FOUND A PLACE I CAN CALL HOME. AND I TAKE IT WITH ME WHEREVER I GO. THANKS, NOMADIC ANIMALS MOBILE HOME DEALERSHIP!

THIS HERMIT CRAB MIGHT TALK A BIG GAME, BUT MAKE NO MISTAKE, HE'S GOT A COUPLE OF SOFT SIDES THAT, IF LEFT EXPOSED, MAKE HIM VULNERABLE TO PREDATORS AND HARSH WEATHER CONDITIONS.

AND DESPITE MY NAME, I'M ACTUALLY QUITE SOCIAL! SO COME ON OVER SOMETIME! JUST DON'T COME **IN**.

HERMIT CRAB

MY LAST NAME, ARMADILLO, LITERALLY TRANSLATES TO "LITTLE ARMORED ONE" IN SPANISH. SO WHEN IT CAME TO A MOBILE HOME, I WANTED TO GET SOMETHING THAT WOULD LIVE UP TO THE FAMILY NAME. LUCKILY, NOMADIC ANIMALS MOBILE HOME DEALERSHIP SET ME UP WITH A SEGMENTED SHELL TO PROTECT ME FROM PREDATORS. BUT THEY ALSO MADE IT FLEXIBLE ENOUGH FOR ME TO LIVE OUT MY DREAMS OF BECOMING A SOCCER BALL!

EACH SHELL IS MADE UP OF BONY PLATES COVERED IN A LAYER OF THICK, HARD SKIN.

AND FOR AN ADDED SECURITY FEATURE, WHEN I CURL UP INTO A BALL, I'LL OFTEN LEAVE A SPACE OPEN. IF A PREDATOR PUTS ITS PAW OR NOSE INTO THAT SPACE TO PRY ME OPEN, I'LL SLAM MY SHELL SHUT. LIKE FINGERS IN A CAR DOOR!

OUCH! I MEAN, GET YOURS TODAY!

THREE-BANDED ARMADILLO

GENERATION CONSERVATION

In 2011, a group of biologists estimated that there are more than 8.7 million species of animals on Earth, but humans have only identified about 1.2 million of them!

A biologist is a scientist who studies life and living organisms like plants and animals.

And a species is a group of organisms—or any living thing—that can reproduce.

Even with *all* of these species on our planet, it's estimated that as many as 150 of them go extinct every single day.

In the past one hundred years alone, our planet has lost some amazing creatures, including:

The western black African rhinoceros: The last one of these creatures was seen in 2006.

The Pyrenean ibex: A relative of the Spanish ibex or Iberian goat, this grass-eating grazer was hunted mainly by humans until none were left. The last Pyrenean ibex died in 2000.

The Tasmanian tiger: This large, meat-eating marsupial lived on the Australian island state of Tasmania and looked like a medium-size dog with tiger stripes! The last of its kind died in captivity in a Tasmanian zoo in 1936.

Other animals are considered to be endangered species. This means that they are at risk of extinction because of a sudden decrease in their population or a loss of their habitat.

Some endangered species include:

The monarch butterfly: The monarch butterfly is one of the most recognizable butterflies in the world, but for decades, their population has been in decline as the milkweed plant has become more scarce. Milkweed is the only plant in which these North American butterflies will lay their eggs and the only plant the caterpillars will eat. Conservationists are relying on citizen scientists like us to help the plight of the monarch butterfly by planting milkweed plants where we can.

Loggerhead sea turtles: An estimated 8.5 million tons of plastic waste winds up in our oceans each year, and it's hurting—and sometimes killing—the sea creatures who call these waters home. One such animal is the loggerhead sea turtle, whose population is in steep decline partly due to the fact that it swallows and becomes tangled up in plastic trash.

The giant panda: One of the rarest animal species in the world, the giant panda spends its days chewing on bamboo stems in the cold mountain forests of Central China. But because these bamboo forests are being cut down for timber and farmland at a rapid rate, the giant panda is losing the habitat and home it needs to survive.

This is horrible! I feel so helpless!

But wait! We can help!

Five Things YOU Can Do to Help Preserve Wildlife on Planet Earth!

1. Call or write your representatives in government! Ask them to support laws that better protect animals. In the United States, the Endangered Species Act has helped to save bald eagles, grizzly bears, and humpback whales—all animals that were on the verge of  extinction in the past. According to the US Fish and Wildlife Service, this law has helped to prevent the extinction of 99 percent of the species it protects!

2. Eat *less* meat! Eat *more* bugs! When we raise livestock (cows, pigs, chickens) for meat, we're also creating more carbon emissions. And the more carbon we create, the warmer our planet will become. A hotter planet means more animals will become extinct. So maybe cut back on meat (or look for sustainably raised beef, pork, and chicken) or consider replacing some meat with insects. Yes, insects! Crickets, for example, provide a plentiful and environmentally friendly source of protein.

3. Buy less stuff! The toys and souvenirs you buy require a lot of energy to produce. And when you buy bottled water at the store, it comes in single-use plastic bottles. By making and reusing things—and drinking tap water at home—you're not only cutting down on plastic waste (which is very hard to recycle), but you're also throwing away less stuff too—stuff that might otherwise wind up in landfills, or even worse, the

ocean. By limiting the amount of stuff you buy, you're helping to keep our sea creatures, our planet, *and* your wallet happy and healthy!

4. Create a new habitat at home! By planting native pollinating plants in your yard or in pots on a stoop or balcony, you can help provide food for birds, bees, butterflies, and other wildlife. And by planting milkweed that's local to your area, you can play a huge role in helping monarch butterflies migrate in the fall! Be sure to check out the National Wildlife Federation's Garden for Wildlife program for more information on how to help with habitat restoration.

5. Learn more about the Half-Earth Project! This is an idea to set aside half of the land on planet Earth for nature—no factories, no cities, no farms, *just animals*. The idea comes from famed biologist E. O. Wilson, who believes if we do this, we could help save 85 percent or more of today's species from extinction!

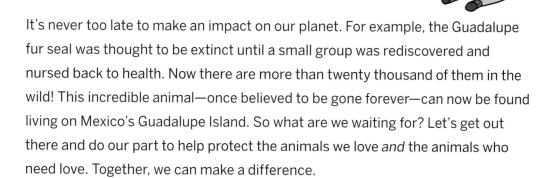

It's never too late to make an impact on our planet. For example, the Guadalupe fur seal was thought to be extinct until a small group was rediscovered and nursed back to health. Now there are more than twenty thousand of them in the wild! This incredible animal—once believed to be gone forever—can now be found living on Mexico's Guadalupe Island. So what are we waiting for? Let's get out there and do our part to help protect the animals we love *and* the animals who need love. Together, we can make a difference.

HIGH FASHION FOR EVERY HABITAT

Animals evolve to adapt to their environments—and so can *you!* Let's hear from some humans who have taken fashion cues from the animal kingdom.

 BEAK

"For years I used an ordinary knife to cut my food. Not anymore! I had this long, colorful toucan beak installed on my face, and now I can tear my food apart hands-free! The only downside is that it makes it hard to smile!"

 **FEATHERS**

"What's my secret to looking fantastic? FEATHERS! And they're not just fancy; they're functional, too! They help me fly, float, and forage for food."

Uh . . . I'm not sure it works that way.

 FUR

"I started saying NO to haircuts! I was inspired by the arctic animals who use fur to keep themselves warm. Once my undercoat grows in, it will help trap body heat."

 GILLS

"I bought these gills, thinking they'd help me breathe underwater like a fish, but it turns out they don't absorb oxygen from water *or* send oxygen to my bloodstream. I want my money back!"

SCALES

"What's my secret? SCALES. I have a closet full of them! Some help me to slink around like a snake and some are like a suit of armor."

WEBBED FEET

"I was given these webbed feet by a duck friend. They allow me to paddle through water and walk on muddy land."

GLOSSARY

Adaptation—an evolutionary process that makes an animal better at doing something.

Amphibian—a group of cold-blooded animals that have backbones and need water or a moist environment in order to live. This group includes frogs, toads, and salamanders.

Antennae—feelers that come out of insects' and crustaceans' heads and help them sense.

Appendage—an external body part such as an antenna or a leg that sticks out and performs a special task.

Arachnid—a group of animals that have jointed limbs and no backbones, including spiders, scorpions, and ticks.

Arthropod—a group of animals that don't have backbones, including insects, spiders, and lobsters.

Avian—anything relating to birds.

Bacteria—single-celled living organisms that are often microscopic and that are very important to the well-being of ecosystems.

Beak—a hard, pointed protrusion at the front of a bird's or octopus's face that's actually an extension of their jaw.

Bioluminescence—the ability of an organism to create light on its own.

Camouflage—a disguise that helps an animal blend into its surroundings.

Canopy—the topmost layer of a forest, where most of its animals live.

Carcass—the dead body of an animal.

Carnivore—an animal that mainly eats meat.

Cephalopod—an underwater animal that has tentacles, like an octopus, squid, or cuttlefish.

Cetacean—a mammal that lives in water, like a dolphin or whale.

Climate change—shifts in the Earth's temperature caused by natural weather patterns and the actions of humans.

Colony—a group of animals from the same species living and interacting together.

Compost—a type of nutrient-rich soil formed from dead plants and animals.

Crustacean—a mostly aquatic group of animals that includes crabs, shrimp, and barnacles.

Decomposition—the process of rotting and decaying that breaks down dead matter.

Dissect—the process of cutting into something in order to study its inner parts.

DNA—the microscopic code that underwrites all living things.

Echolocation—an animal's ability to sense its environment by bouncing sound off its surroundings.

Ecosystem—a network consisting of animals and their environment.

Ectotherm—cold-blooded, or an animal that gets heat from the outside world.

Endotherm—warm-blooded, or an animal that can stay warm in a cold environment.

Environment—the space in which an animal lives and roams.

Exoskeleton—a tough covering that supports and protects animals that don't have backbones, like insects.

Extinction—the death of every animal in a group, usually a species.

Feathers—light, often colorful growths that cover birds and keep them warm.

Fossil—the preserved remains of a dead organism, often bones or an impression in rock.

Gill—an organ that allows aquatic animals like fish and tadpoles to breathe underwater.

Habitat—the natural home of an animal.

Hatchling—a very young animal that has recently come out of an egg.

Herbivore—an animal that only eats plants.

Incubate—the process of sitting on top of eggs to keep them warm until they hatch.

Insectivore—an animal or plant that eats insects.

Invertebrate—an animal that doesn't have a backbone.

Larvae—young animals, often insects, that have hatched out of an egg and will undergo metamorphosis to become adults. Caterpillars and maggots are both types of larvae.

Lineage—a line of related animals that are direct descendants of one another.

Livestock—farm animals like cows, pigs, and horses.

Mammal—a group of warm-blooded animals that have backbones and feed milk to their young. This group includes cows, platypuses, and humans.

Mandible—the crushing bone near an arthropod's mouth that helps it fight other animals and grab and chew food.

Metamorphosis—the process by which a larva transforms into an adult. A tadpole becoming a frog is an example of metamorphosis.

Monotreme—a group of mammals that includes echidnas and platypuses.

Nectar—a sugary liquid produced in or near the flower of a plant to attract pollinating animals.

Nocturnal—sleeping during the day and staying awake at night.

Nymphs—young insects that have hatched out of an egg but don't go through metamorphosis to become adults.

Omnivore—an animal that eats both plants and meat.

Opposable thumbs—thumbs that point in the opposite direction of the fingers near them, helping an animal grab and hold objects.

Paleontologist—a scientist who studies fossils.

Parasite—an animal that feeds off another animal and hurts it in the process.

Plankton—tiny organisms that float through water and are eaten by fish, whales, and other marine animals.

Plumage—all the feathers of a bird.

Predator—an animal that hunts and eats another animal.

Prey—an animal that is hunted and eaten by another animal.

Reptile—a group of cold-blooded animals that have scales and backbones and that lay eggs. This group includes snakes, lizards, and turtles.

Rodent—a group of mammals that gnaw, including rats, mice, rabbits, and porcupines.

Scute—a thick plate, the kind that makes up part of a turtle's shell or lines the back of a crocodile.

Skeletonization—the process by which something dead becomes a pile of bones.

Spawn—the eggs and sperm that aquatic animals deposit into water in order to reproduce.

Species—a group of highly related animals, such as house cats or beluga whales.

Symbiotic—an interaction between two animals wherein both benefit.

Tentacles—arms that some aquatic animals have, which they use for grasping, sensing, and feeding.

Thermoregulation—an animal's ability to keep itself warm or cold without relying on heat from the outside world.

Tropical—areas (especially forests) that are sunnier, hotter, and wetter than most other parts of the Earth.

Venomous—the ability of an animal to bite or sting, which is dangerous to humans.

Vertebrate—an animal that has a backbone.

Whiskers—stiff hairs that some animals have that help them sense their environment.

Wingspan—the distance from the tip of a bird's wing all the way to the tip of its other wing.

Yolk—the yellow inside of a bird's egg.

BIBLIOGRAPHY AND RECOMMENDED READING

Atkins, Marcie Flinchum. *Wait, Rest, Pause*. Minneapolis, MN: Millbrook Press, 2019.

Burnie, David. *The Animal Book*. New York: DK, 2013.

Clarke, Ginjer. *The Fascinating Animal Book for Kids*. Emeryville, CA: Rockridge Press, 2020.

Dorion, Christine. *Invented by Animals: Meet the Creatures Who Inspired Our Everyday Technology*. London, UK: Wide-Eyed Editions, 2021.

Fleming, Candace, and Eric Rohmann. *Honeybee: The Busy Life of* Apis Mellifera. New York, NY: Holiday House, 2020.

Isabella, Jude, and Kim Smith. *Bringing Back the Wolves: How a Predator Restored an Ecosytem*. Toronto, ON: Kids Can Press, 2020.

Lloyd, Christopher. *Humanimal*. Greenbelt, MD: What on Earth Publishing, 2019.

Murawski, Darlyne, and Nancy Honovich. *Ultimate Bugopedia*. Washington, DC: National Geographic, 2013.

Radeva, Sabina. *Charles Darwin's* On the Origin of Species. New York: Crown Books for Young Readers, 2019.

Rothery, Ben. *Hidden Planet: Secrets of the Animal Kingdom*. Thomaston, ME: Tilbury House Publishing, 2021.

Shreeve, Elizabeth. *Out of the Blue: How Animals Evolved from Prehistoric Seas*. Illustrated by Frann Preston-Gannon. Somerville, MA: Candlewick, 2021.

Sidman, Joyce. *The Girl Who Drew Butterflies: How Maria Merian's Art Changed Science*. Boston: Houghton Mifflin Harcourt, 2018.

Spelman, Lucy. *Animal Encyclopedia*. Washington, DC: National Geographic, 2012.

Special thanks to our Wow in the World librarian, Kit Ballenger (@KitonLit), for these additional book recommendations.

RECOMMENDED LISTENING

But wait—there's more! We've got some recommended listening for your earballs. Have your grownup scan these QR codes to listen to some of our favorite *wild* episodes of *Wow in the World*!

Orange Is the New Bat

Tell Me How You Really Eel

What's Slower Than Slow?

The Trouble with Pterosaur

The Cubic Scoop on Wombat Poop!

Sea Slug Style

Growling Ghost-Crabs

Nice-off! Cats vs. Dogs

Rat-a-Tat Tickle Attack

Need to Settle a Dispute? Try Venom!

Slingshot Spider

The Mysterious Case of the Missing Salmon

SOURCE NOTES

Introduction

Scientists estimate that: Richard Black, "Species Count Put at 8.7 Million," *BBC News*, August 23, 2011 (www.bbc.com/news/science-environment-14616161, August 2, 2020).

Part I. Feathered Friends

Partly hollow: Elizabeth R. Dumont, "Bone Density and the Lightweight Skeletons of Birds," *Proceedings of the Royal Society of Biological Sciences* 277, no. 6 (July 2010): 2193–98.

Birds are the only: The Cornell Lab, "What Makes a Bird . . . A Bird?" (www.birds.cornell.edu/k12/september, August 4, 2020).

Their beaks serve: A. Abzhanov et al., "Bmp4 and Morphological Variation of Beaks in Darwin's Finches," *Science* 305, no. 5689 (September 2004): 1462–65.

Fanciful Flight: Bret W. Tobalske, "Biomechanics of Bird Flight," *Journal of Experimental Biology* 210 (2007): 3135–46.

Built-in Raincoat: Peter Cotgreave and Dale H. Clayton, "Comparative Analysis of Time Spent Grooming by Birds in Relation to Parasite Load," *Behaviour* 131, no. 3/4 (1994): 171–87.

And an Umbrella: Shweta Karikehalli, "Watch a Black Heron Fool Fish by Turning Into an Umbrella," *Audubon*, January 17, 2019 (www.audubon.org/news/watch-black-heron-fool-fish-turning-umbrella, August 5, 2020).

Camouflage: Kila Davis and Denver W. Holt, *Owls, Whoo Are They?* Missoula: Mountain Press, 1996.

We're looking at you: K. Koskenpato et al., "Gray Plumage Color Is More Cryptic Than Brown in Snowy Landscapes in a Resident Color Polymorphic Bird," *Ecology and Evolution* 10, no. 4 (February 2020): 1751–61.

Did you know: Christopher J. Clark et al., "Smithornis Broadbills Produce Loud Wing Song by Aeroelastic Flutter of Medial Primary Wing Feathers," *Journal of Experimental Biology* 219 (2016): 1069–75.

Use them for: Jason Bittel, "These Birds Can Sing Using Only Their Feathers," *Smithsonian*, April 8, 2016 (www.smithsonianmag.com/science-nature/these-birds-can-sing-using-only-their-feathers-180958678, August 10, 2020).

Use your feathers to: Lesley Evans Ogden, "The Silent Flight of Owls, Explained," *Audubon*, July 28, 2017 (www.audubon.org/news/the-silent-flight-owls-explained, August 5, 2020).

Digestion: Paul R. Ehrlich, David S. Dobkin, and Darryl Wheye, "Eating Feathers," Birds of Stanford (web.stanford.edu/group/stanfordbirds/text/essays/Eating_Feathers.html, August 5, 2020).

Home Decorating: Paul R. Ehrlich, David S. Dobkin, and Darryl Wheye, "Feathered Nests," Birds of Stanford (web.stanford.edu/group/stanfordbirds/text/essays/Eating_Feathers.html, August 5, 2020).

Can dive at speeds: Guinness World Records Limited, "Fastest Bird (Diving)," 2005 (www.guinnessworldrecords.com/world-records/70929-fastest-bird-diving, August 6, 2020).

Lifespan: National Geographic, "Peregrine Falcon" (www.nationalgeographic.com/animals/birds/p/peregrine-falcon/#close, August 6, 2020).

The Albatross: National Geographic, "Albatross" (www.nationalgeographic.com/animals/birds/group/albatrosses, August 6, 2020).

Can travel up to: Kennedy Warne, "The Amazing Albatrosses," *Smithsonian*, September 2007 (www.smithsonianmag.com/science-nature/the-amazing-albatrosses-162515529, August 6, 2020).

Serviceable routes: National Geographic, "Arctic Tern" (www.nationalgeographic.com/animals/birds/a/arctic-tern, August 6, 2020).

He's a cassowary: San Diego Zoo, "Cassowary" (animals.sandiegozoo.org/animals/cassowary, August 6, 2020).

Plus you can lay: San Diego Zoo, "Southern Cassowary" (animals.sandiegozoo.org/animals/cassowary, August 6, 2020).

Look at you: Catherine D. Hughes, "Ostrich Facts!," National Geographic Kids (www.natgeokids.com/nz/discover/animals/birds/ostrich-facts, August 6, 2020).

But you can still: San Diego Zoo, "Emu" (www.animals.sandiegozoo.org/animals/emu, August 6, 2020).

You're practically the jackrabbit: Mary Bates, "10 Fun Facts About the Kakapo," *Wired*, March 4, 2014 (www.wired.com/2014/03/creature-feature-10-fun-facts-kakapo, August 6, 2020).

And you're the only *bird*: The Kiwi Trust, "An Unusual Beak," Kiwis for Kiwi (www.kiwisforkiwi.org/about-kiwi/kiwi-facts-characteristics/an-unusual-beak, August 6, 2020).

Is he hoping that: San Diego Zoo, "Bowerbird" (www.animals.sandiegozoo.org/animals/bowerbird, August 6, 2020).

Let's give it up: S. Hoffmann et al., "Duets Recorded in the Wild Reveal That Interindividually Coordinated Motor Control Enables Cooperative Behavior," *Nature Communications* 10, no. 2577 (2019) (www.nature.com/articles/s41467-019-10593-3, August 6, 2020).

"Anting": Thomas Eisner and Daniel Aneshansley, "'Anting' in Blue Jays," *Chemoecology* 18, no. 4 (2008): 197–203.

Scientists are still: Eric Grundhauser, "Birds Rub Ants on Themselves, and No One Knows Exactly Why," Atlas Obscura, November 21, 2017 (www.atlasobscura.com/articles/mystery-bird-anting, August 5, 2020).

"I hoard acorns": Kenn Kaufman, "Acorn Woodpecker," Audubon (www.audubon.org/field-guide/bird/acorn-woodpecker, August 7, 2020).

They've been known, Animal World and Snake Farm Zoo, "Raven" (www.awsfzoo.com/exhibit/raven, August 6, 2020).

The Haystack: San Diego Zoo, "Sociable Weaver (animals.sandiegozoo.org/animals/sociable-weaver, August 6, 2020).

A Gardener's Dream: National Malleefowl Recovery Team, "Malleefowl Facts" (www.nationalmalleefowl.com.au/about/malleefowl-facts, August 5, 2020).

A Crafter's Delight: Birds in Backyards, "Golden-Headed Cisticola" (www.birdsinbackyards.net/species/Cisticola-exilis, August 6, 2020).

The Outdoor Oven: Felipe L. S. Shibuya, Talita V. Braga, and James J. Roper, "The Rufous Hornero (*Furnarius Rufus*) Nest as an Incubation Chamber," *Journal of Thermal Biology* 47 (2015): 7–12.

The largest egg: Alina Bradford, "Ostrich Facts: The World's Largest Bird," Live Science, September 17, 2014 (www.livescience.com/27433-ostriches.html, August 6, 2020).

The smallest known egg: Guinness World Records Limited, "The Smallest Egg," 1998 (www.guinnessworldrecords.com/world-records/smallest-bird-egg, August 7, 2020).

As a hen gets older: L. V. Anderson, "Small Eggs Taste Much Better Than Large Eggs. Why Is It So Hard to Find Them?," Slate, January 13, 2014 (slate.com/culture/2014/01/small-eggs-taste-better-large-eggs-are-more-common-so-freshdirect-introduces-farmers-eggs-aka-pullet-eggs.html, August 7, 2020).

About five thousand years: Tamar Hodos, "Eggstraordinary artefacts: decorated ostrich eggs in the ancient Mediterranean world," *Humanities and Social Sciences Communications* 7, no. 45 (2020) (www.nature.com/articles/s41599-020-00541-8, August 7, 2020).

About one in a thousand: Deirdre Toher, "Scrambled Statistics: What Are the Chances of Finding Multi-Yolk Eggs?," *Significance Magazine* (August 2016): 11.

Chickens with white: Joe Schwarcz, "You Can Determine the Colour of an Egg a Chicken Lays by Looking at It's Earlobe," McGill Office for Science and Society, April 18, 2019 (www.mcgill.ca/oss/article/did-you-know-nutrition/you-can-determine-colour-egg-looking-chickens-earlobe, August 12, 2020).

To tell if an egg: Science Buddies, Sabine De Brabandere, "Raw or Cooked? That Is the Question!," *Scientific American*, April 25, 2019 (www.scientificamerican.com/article/raw-or-cooked-that-is-the-question, August 8, 2020).

Cowbirds and common cuckoos: Rebecca Croston and Mark E. Hauber, "The Ecology of Avian Brood Parasitism," *Nature Education Knowledge* 3, no. 10 (2010): 56.

It's a biological cycle: Libbie Johnson, "Factors That Affect Egg Production in Chickens," University of Florida, February 27, 2015 (nwdistrict.ifas.ufl.edu/phag/2015/02/27/factors-that-affect-egg-production-in-chickens, August 7, 2020).

Many consider the archaeopteryx: Martin Kundrát et al., "The First Specimen of Archaeopteryx from the Upper Jurassic Mörnsheim Formation of Germany," *Historical Biology* 39, no. 1 (2019): 3–63.

The male peacock: Cosley Zoo, "India Blue Peafowl" (cosleyzoo.org/india-blue-peafowl, August 4, 2020).

Bird's nest soup: Benjamin Graham, "Bird's Nest Soup Is More Popular Than Ever, Thanks to Swiftlet House Farms," Audubon, October 23, 2017 (www.audubon.org/news/birds-nest-soup-more-popular-ever-thanks-swiftlet-house-farms, August 5, 2020).

New Caledonian crows: Antone Martinho III et al., "Monocular Tool Control, Eye Dominance, and Laterality in New Caledonian Crows," *Current Biology* 24, no. 24 (2014): 2930–34.

The pileated woodpecker: The Cornell Lab, "Pileated Woodpecker," All About Birds (www.allaboutbirds.org/guide/Pileated_Woodpecker/lifehistory#, August 5, 2020).

A woodpecker can: Yuzhe Liu et al., "Response of Woodpecker's Head during Pecking Process Simulated by Material Point Method," *PLoS One* 10, no. 4 (2015) (www.ncbi.nlm.nih.gov/pmc/articles/PMC4406624, August 5, 2020).

Ostriches' eyes are: Katie Pavid, "Amazing Eyes: 17 Vision Champions," Natural History Museum UK (www.nhm.ac.uk/discover/amazing-eyes-vision-champions.html, August 5, 2020).

One bar-tailed godwit: Daniel Boffey, "'Jet Fighter' Godwit Breaks World Record for Non-stop Bird Flight," *Guardian*, October 13, 2020 (www.theguardian.com/environment/2020/oct/13/jet-fighter-godwit-breaks-world-record-for-non-stop-bird-flight, August 7, 2020).

A waddle of: Abigail Pietrow, "What Do You Call a Group of Penguins?," Penguins International, November 17, 2020 (www.penguinsinternational.org/2020/11/17/what-do-you-call-a-group-of-penguins, January 2, 2021).

A murder of: PBS, "Crow Facts," Nature, February 21, 2013 (www.pbs.org/wnet/nature/a-murder-of-crows-crow-facts/5965, January 2, 2021).

A flamboyance of: Alan Taylor, "A Flamboyance of Flamingos," *Atlantic*, May 19, 2020 (www.theatlantic.com/photo/2020/05/photos-a-flamboyance-of-flamingos/611848, January 2, 2021).

A dropping of: Le Nichoir, "Collective Nouns" (lenichoir.org/collective-nouns, January 2, 2021).

And he's going to have: San Diego Zoo, "Flamingo" (animals.sandiegozoo.org/animals/flamingo, January 4, 2021).

As it turns out: Paul Rose, "Africa's Most Toxic Lakes Are a Paradise for Fearless Flamingos," The Conversation, January 5, 2017 (theconversation.com/africas-most-toxic-lakes-are-a-paradise-for-fearless-flamingos-70817, January 4, 2021).

As one of the largest: San Diego Zoo, "Harpy Eagle" (animals.sandiegozoo.org/animals/harpy-eagle, January 4, 2021).

Eurasian roller bird: D. Parejo et al., "Rollers Smell the Fear of Nestlings," *Biology Letters* 8, no. 4 (2012) (royalsocietypublishing.org/doi/10.1098/rsbl.2012.0124, August 5, 2020).

Help Wanted

With over two thousand years: Pigeon Control Resource Centre, "Pigeons—Everything There Is to Know about the Pigeon" (www.pigeoncontrolresourcecentre.org/html/about-pigeons.html#topofpage, August 5, 2020).

Requirements: A keen sense: Tim Guilford, "Explainer: How Do Homing Pigeons Navigate?," The Conversation, August 23, 2014 (theconversation.com/explainer-how-do-homing-pigeons-navigate-25633, August 6, 2020).

This job will require you: Apopo, "Herorats Save Lives" (www.apopo.org/en/herorats/herorats-save-lives, August 5, 2020).

Part II. Reptile Style

And while we celebrate: Peter Uetz, "Species Statistics," Reptile Database, September 22, 2020 (www.reptile-database.org/db-info/SpeciesStat.html, October 12, 2020).

Endothermic animals: Audubon, "How Do Birds Cope with Cold in Winter" (www.audubon.org/how-do-birds-cope-cold-winter, October 5, 2020).

They're also able to help: UMPC Department of Neurosurgery, "Staying Warm in Cold Weather—Thanks to Your Brain," Health Beat, December 27, 2013 (share.upmc.com/2013/12/your-brain-and-cold-weather/?vwo=header_redesign, October 5, 2020).

We took an ancestry test: CK-12 Foundation, "Reptile Evolution," CK-12 Biology Concepts, August 15, 2020 (bio.libretexts.org/Bookshelves/Introductory_and_General_Biology/Book%3A_Introductory_Biology_(CK-12)/12%3A_Vertebrates/12.19%3A_Reptile_Evolution, October 4, 2020).

In fact, Great-Great-Grandma: National Geographic, "Galapagos Tortoise" (www.nationalgeographic.com/animals/reptiles/g/galapagos-tortoise, October 4, 2020).

Anyone who has ever spent: Masaya Iijima, Tai Kubo, and Yoshitsugu Kobayashi, "Comparative Limb Proportions Reveal Differential Locomotor Morphofunctions of Alligatoroids and Crocodyloids," *Royal Society Open Science* 5, no. 3 (2018) (royalsocietypublishing.org/doi/full/10.1098/rsos.171774, October 8, 2020).

And you'll NEVER: USGS, "Do Alligators and Crocodiles Exist Together Anywhere in the World?" (www.usgs.gov/faqs/do-alligators-and-crocodiles-exist-together-anywhere-world?qt-news_science_products=0#qt-news_science_products, October 5, 2020).

They can't chew: Stephanie K. Drumheller, James Darlington, and Kent A. Vliet, "Surveying Death Roll Behavior across Crocodylia," *Ethology Ecology and Evolution* 31, no. 4 (2019): 329–47.

The Chinese softshell: Michael Marshall, "Zoologger: The turtle That Urinates through Its Mouth," *New Scientist*, October 11, 2012 (www.newscientist.com/article/dn22365-zoologger-the-turtle-that-urinates-through-its-mouth, October 12, 2020).

And speaking of: Brian Handwerk, "It's Not Just Bears," *National Geographic*, March 7, 2019 (nationalgeographic.com/animals/2019/03/animals-winter-hibernation-turtles, October 8, 2020).

This is how they: Jérémie Teyssier et al., "Photonic Crystals Cause Active Colour Change in Chameleons," *Nature Communications* 6 (2015) (www.nature.com/articles/ncomms7368, October 8, 2020).

Some cobras can: Bruce A. Young, Melissa Boetig, and Guido Westhoff, "Functional Bases of the Spatial Dispersal of Venom during Cobra 'Spitting,'" *Physiological and Biochemical Zoology* 82, no. 1 (2009): 80–89.

In 2014, a cobra: Matt Cantor, "Cobra's severed head bites, kills chef," USA TODAY, August 26, 2014 (www.usatoday.com/story/news/world/2014/08/26/newser-cobra-kills-chef/14619677, August 8, 2020).

At a hair salon: Von Jürgen Helfricht, "Bei diesem Friseur arbeitet eine Würgeschlange," Bild, March 1, 2017 (www.bild.de/regional/dresden/friseur/bei-diesem-friseur-arbeitet-eine-wuergeschlange-50644908.bild.html, October 8, 2020).

Paleontologists discovered: Federico Fanti et al., "The largest thalattosuchian (Crocodylomorpha) supports teleosaurid survival across the Jurassic-Cretaceous boundary," *Cretaceous Research* 61 (2016): 263–74.

Rattlesnakes add new: National Geographic, "Rattlesnake," National Geographic Kids (kids.nationalgeographic.com/animals/reptiles/rattlesnake/=, October 8, 2020).

Australia's thorny devil: Philipp Comanns et al., "Cutaneous water collection by a moisture-harvesting lizard, the thorny devil (Moloch horridus)," *Journal of Experimental Biology* 219 (2016): 3473–79.

Twenty-one of the twenty-five: Cayla Dengate, Australia Is Home to Heaps of the World's 25 Most Venomous Snakes," HuffPost, September 3, 2016 (www.huffingtonpost.com.au/2016/03/08/venomous-snakes-australia_n_9413542.html, October 8, 2020).

A tangled knot: Andrea DenHoed, "A Rhumba of Rattlesnakes, a Shakespeare Originalist," *The New Yorker*, September 6, 2013 (www.newyorker.com/books/page-turner/weekend-reading-a-rhumba-of-rattlesnakes-a-shakespeare-originalist, October 8, 2020).

What to Expect: University of Florida, "The Croc Docs" (crocdoc.ifas.ufl.edu/publications/fieldtrips/nestingcrocodiles, October 8, 2020).

No bibs to put on: World Wildlife Federation, "Crocodile Facts" (www.nathab.com/know-before-you-go/african-safaris/southern-africa/wildlife-guide/crocodile, October 8, 2020).

The Animal Avengers Series

Watch in amazement: Amina Khan, "Sea cucumbers have a secret superpower," Popular Science, April 20, 2017 (www.popsci.com/secret-superpower-sea-cucumbers, October 8, 2020).

This backward-aging jellyfish: Alyssa Navarro, Tech Times, March 6, 2016 (www.techtimes.com/articles/138945/20160306/moon-jellyfish-age-backwards-just-like-benjamin-button.htm, October 8, 2020).

The Maniacal Mantis: Wei Huang, "A natural impact-resistant bicontinuous composite nanoparticle coating," *Nature Materials* 19 (2020): 1236–43.

Shockwaves of up to: National Geographic, "Electric Eel" (www.nationalgeographic.com/animals/fish/e/electric-eel, August 8, 2020).

I heard its body: Fox Meyer, "How Octopuses and Squids Change Color," October 2013 (ocean.si.edu/ocean-life/invertebrates/how-octopuses-and-squids-change-color, October 8, 2020).

Part III. Magnificent Mammals

Marsupials, mammals commonly: Australian Museum, "What Is a Marsupial?," November 2, 2018 (australian.museum/learn/species-identification/ask-an-expert/what-is-a-marsupial, October 20, 2020).

The word marsupial: Merriam-Webster, "Marsupium" (www.merriam-webster.com/dictionary/marsupium, October 20, 2020).

The short-tailed: Teresa Bradley Bays, Teresa Lightfoot, and Jörg Mayer, eds. *Exotic Pet Behavior*. St. Louis: Saunders Elsevier, 2006.

This keeps my: National Geographic, "Opossums" (www.nationalgeographic.com/animals/mammals/group/opossums, October 20, 2020).

And since my pouch: Australian Koala Foundation, "Physical Characteristics of the Koala" (www.savethekoala.com/about-koalas/physical-characteristics-koala, October 8, 2020).

Just like pregnant: Alina Bradford, "Kangaroo Facts," Live Science, March 2, 2016 (www.livescience.com/27400-kangaroos.html, October 8, 2020).

And she cleans it: C. Claiborne Ray, "Marsupial Maintenance," The New York Times, August 13, 2012 (www.nytimes.com/2012/08/14/science/how-do-female-kangaroos-keep-their-pouches-clean.html, October 6, 2020).

This could take: City Wildlife, "The Truth about Opossums," April 24, 2015 (citywildlife.org/the-truth-about-opossums, October 8, 2020).

The platypus: Lauren Thomas, "Monotremes, Marsupials, and Placentals," UC Santa Cruz Kenneth S. Norris Center for Natural History, 2017 (norriscenter.ucsc.edu/collections-and-resources/mammals/monotremes-marsupials-placentals.html, October 8, 2020).

WE HAVE LITTLE: UCL, "Monotremata—monotremes," Vertebrate Diversity" (www.ucl.ac.uk/museums-static/obl4he/vertebratediversity/monotremes.html, October 8, 2020).

The only monotremes: UC Museum of Paleontology, "Monotremes," UC Berkeley (ucmp.berkeley.edu/mammal/monotreme.html, October 8, 2020).

The word monotreme: K.W.S. Ashwell, "The Nervous Systems of Early Mammals and Their Evolution," *Evolution of Nervous Systems*. Cambridge: Academic Press, 2017.

Since they share: Ann Gibbons, "Bonobos Join Chimps as Closest Human Relatives," Science, June 13, 2012 (www.sciencemag.org/news/2012/06/bonobos-join-chimps-closest-human-relatives, October 10, 2020).

Whales know that: NOAA, "Why do whales make sounds?," National Ocean Service, April 6, 2020 (oceanservice.noaa.gov/facts/whalesounds.html, October 12, 2020).

Scientists believe that: Eyder Peralta, "Researcher: Sperm Whales Might Give Each Other Names," NPR, March 14, 2011 (www.npr.org/sections/thetwo-way/2011/03/14/134534139/researcher-sperm-whales-might-give-each-other-names, October 8, 2020).

Thanks to research: Bec Crew, "Catch the Wave: Decoding the Prairie Dog's Contagious Jump-Yips," *Scientific American*, January 7, 2014 (blogs.scientificamerican.com/running-ponies/catch-the-wave-decoding-the-prairie-doge28099s-contagious-jump-yips, October 12, 2020).

That's right: Allan Adamson, "Pet Translator: Scientist Developing Device To Convert Dog Barks Into English Language," Tech Times, January 15, 2018 (www.techtimes.com/articles/218841/20180115/pet-translator-scientist-developing-device-to-convert-dog-barks-into-english-language.htm, October 12, 2020).

If you add them: Guy Musser, "Rodent," Brittanica, April 4, 2020 (www.britannica.com/animal/rodent, October 12, 2020).

Rodents come in: Patrick Sherman, "Cardiocranius paradoxus," Animal Diversity Web, 2007 (animaldiversity.org/accounts/Cardiocranius_paradoxus, October 12, 2020).

These chompers give: Melissa Rouge, "Dental Anatomy of Rodents," Colorado State University (www.vivo.colostate.edu/hbooks/pathphys/digestion/pregastric/rodentpage.html, August 8, 2020).

Predators beware: African Wildlife Foundation, "Porcupine" (www.awf.org/wildlife-conservation/porcupine, October 12, 2020).

The capybara is: National Geographic, "Capybara" (www.nationalgeographic.com/animals/mammals/c/cabybara-facts, August 8, 2020).

It hails from: San Diego Zoo, "Capybara" (animals.sandiegozoo.org/animals/capybara, August 8, 2020).

It's a rodent: African Wildlife Foundation, "Springhare" (www.awf.org/wildlife-conservation/springhare).

The beaver is: National Geographic, "Beaver" (www.nationalgeographic.com/animals/mammals/b/beaver, August 8, 2020).

Folds of stretchy skin: National Wildlife Federation, "Flying Squirrels" (www.nwf.org/educational-resources/wildlife-guide/mammals/flying-squirrels, August 8, 2020).

They're super versatile: LeeAnn Bies and Phil Myers, "Horns and Antlers," Animal Diversity Web, 2021 (animaldiversity.org/collections/mammal_anatomy/horns_and_antlers, January 12, 2021).

Horns can help: Charles R. Taylor, "The Vascularity and Possible Thermoregulatory Function of the Horns in Goats," *Physiological Zoology* 39, no. 2 (1966): 127–39.

While horns are: Nilanga Jayasinghe, "Where Do Rhinos Live? And Eight Other Rhino Facts," World Wildlife Fund, September 19, 2019 (www.worldwildlife.org/stories/where-do-rhinos-live-and-eight-other-rhino-facts, August 8, 2020).

These massive horns: Alina Bradford, "Buffalo Facts | Water Buffalo & Cape Buffalo," Live Science, July 31, 2014 (www.livescience.com/27409-buffalo.html, August 9, 2020).

Giraffe horns are: Giraffe Conservation Foundation, "Do all giraffe have horns?" (giraffeconservation.org/facts/do-all-giraffe-have-horns, August 9, 2020).

These horns can grow: San Diego Zoo, "Oryx" (animals.sandiegozoo.org/animals/oryx, August 9, 2020).

The male musk ox: Hattie Hayeck, "Everything You Need to Know about the Musk Ox," Discover Wildlife (www.discoverwildlife.com/animal-facts/mammals/facts-about-musk-ox, August 9, 2020).

Male horns can: National Geographic, "Bighorn Sheep" (www.nationalgeographic.com/animals/mammals/b/bighorn-sheep, August 9, 2020).

In fact, it's the only animal: San Diego Zoo, "Wombat" (animals.sandiegozoo.org/animals/wombat, August 9, 2020).

It's called pap feeding: Encyclopedia Britannica, "Koala," Britannica, May 28, 2020 (www.britannica.com/animal/koala, August 9, 2020).

They can't eat: Helen Thompson, "What Drives a Sloth's Ritualistic Trek to Poop?," Smithsonian, January 22, 2014 (www.smithsonianmag.com/science-nature/what-drives-a-sloths-ritualistic-trek-to-poop-180949419, August 9, 2020).

It's a symbiotic: Milla Suutari et al., "Molecular Evidence for a Diverse Green Algal Community Growing in the Hair of Sloths and a Specific Association with *Trichophilus welckeri* (Chlorophyta, Ulvophyceae)," *BMC Ecology and Evolution* 10, no. 86 (2010) (bmcecolevol.biomedcentral.com/articles/10.1186/1471-2148-10-86#citeas, August 10, 2020).

When threatened by: Mark Hay, "A Whale Blasted an Ungodly Amount of A** Ham All Over Some Divers," VICE, January 23, 2015 (www.vice.com/en/article/nnqp4z/a-whale-blasted-an-ungodly-amount-of-ass-ham-all-over-some-divers, August 10, 2020).

And what goes in: San Diego Zoo, "Giant Pandas" (animals.sandiegozoo.org/animals/giant-panda, August 20, 2020).

The rest comes: Elahe Izadi, "Why Giant Pandas Have to Eat and Poop All Day," *Washington Post*, May 20, 2015 (www.washingtonpost.com/[. . .all]?all=news&all=speaking-of-science&all=wp&all=2015&all=05&all=20&all=giant-pandas-somehow-exist-despite-having-guts-that-can-barely-process-the-only-food-they-eat, August 15, 2020).

Known for its: Smithsonian, "Cheetah," Smithsonian National Zoo & Conservation Biology Institute (nationalzoo.si.edu/animals/cheetah, August 15, 2020).

World's Slowest Mammal: Eduardo Garcia, "It's Official: Three-Toed Sloths Are the Slowest Mammals on Earth," *Scientific American*, November 1, 2016 (www.scientificamerican.com/article/it-s-official-three-toed-sloths-are-the-slowest-mammals-on-earth, August 10, 2020).

Central and South America: National Geographic, "Three-Toed Sloths" (www.nationalgeographic.com/animals/mammals/group/three-toed-sloths, August 10, 2020).

Living life in: One Kind Planet, "Three-Toed Sloth" (onekindplanet.org/animal/sloth-three-toed, August 10, 2020).

The tallest giraffe: Adam Millward, "Say HIGH to Forest: Guinness World Records Reveals the World's Tallest Giraffe," Guinness World Records Limited, July 30, 2020 (www.guinnessworldrecords.com/news/2020/7/say-high-to-forest-guinness-world-records-reveals-the-worlds-tallest-giraffe-625257, August 12, 2020).

Tied with the bumblebee bat: Melissa Berg, "A Miniscule Model for Research," *Lab Animal* 45, no. 133 (2016) (www.nature.com/articles/laban.981, August 12, 2020).

World's Biggest Land Mammal: National Geographic, "African Elephant" (www.nationalgeographic.com/animals/mammals/a/african-elephant, August 12, 2020).

Weighing in at: Bas Huijbregts, "African Elephant," World Wildlife Fund (www.worldwildlife.org/species/african-elephant, August 15, 2020).

World Champion of Blowing: National Geographic, "Blue Whale" (www.nationalgeographic.com/animals/mammals/b/blue-whale, August 12, 2020).

Blue whales can: Ella Davies, "The World's Loudest Animal Might Surprise You," BBC, April 1, 2016 (www.bbc.com/earth/story/20160331-the-worlds-loudest-animal-might-surprise-you, August 12, 2020).

The Scottish highlands: What's the Weather Like? "The Climate of Scotland" (www.whatstheweatherlike.org/scotland, August 12, 2020).

Bactrian Camel: Dorling Kindersley, "Mammal Fur and Hair," DK Find Out! (www.dkfindout.com/us/animals-and-nature/mammals/mammal-fur-and-hair, August 12, 2020).

The Pink Pages

It's perhaps the most: Ibrahim Sawal, "Why Are Flamingos Pink," *New Scientist* (www.newscientist.com/question/why-are-flamingos-pink, August 12, 2020).

While the pink: Galapagos Conservation Trust, "Galapagos Pink Land Iguana" (galapagosconservation.org.uk/wildlife/galapagos-pink-land-iguana, August 12, 2020).

Scientists believe the: National Geographic, "Amazon River Dolphin" (www.nationalgeographic.com/animals/mammals/a/amazon-river-dolphin, August 12, 2020).

And because these: Jason Daley, "Adelie Penguins Poop So Much, Their Feces Can Be Seen From Space," *Smithsonian Magazine*, December 13, 2018 (www.smithsonianmag.com/smart-news/how-watching-poo-space-revealing-history-antarcticas-penguins-180971031, August 12, 2020).

Originally, all pigs: Hai-Tian, "Are Pigs All Pink?," *The University of Melbourne Scientific Scribbles*, September 23, 2019 (blogs.unimelb.edu.au/sciencecommunication/2019/09/23/are-pigs-all-pink, August 20, 2020).

It wasn't even discovered: Oceana, "Pygmy Seahorse" (oceana.org/marine-life/ocean-fishes/pygmy-seahorse, August 20, 2020).

The green and pink: Amy Lewis, "Elephant Hawk-Moth: Caterpillar, Lifecycle and Is It Poisonous?," Woodland Trust, July 3, 2018 (www.woodlandtrust.org.uk/blog/2018/07/elephant-hawk-moths, August 20, 2020).

The Naked Mole-Rat: San Diego Zoo, "Naked Mole Rat" (animals.sandiegozoo.org/animals/naked-mole-rat, August 20, 2020).

The Pink Fairy Armadillo: Matt Simon, "Absurd Creature of the Week: Pink Fairy Armadillo Crawls Out of the Desert and into Your Heart," *Wired*, January 3, 2014 (www.wired.com/2014/01/absurd-creature-of-the-week-pink-fairy-armadillo-crawls-out-of-the-desert-and-into-our-hearts, August 20, 2020).

Part IV. Sassy Sea Creatures

Here you'll find: National Geographic, "Fish Pictures and Facts" (www.nationalgeographic.com/animals/fish, September 13, 2020).

No one has: Kinya G. Ota et al., "Identification of Vertebra-Like Elements and Their Possible Differentiation from Sclerotomes in the Hagfish," *Nature Communications* 2, no. 373 (2011) (www.ncbi.nlm.nih.gov/pmc/articles/PMC3157150, September 13, 2020).

About four hundred million years: Nicholas St. Fleur, "Where Did Fish First Evolve? The Answer May Be Shallow," *New York Times*, October 25, 2018 (www.nytimes.com/2018/10/25/science/fish-evolution-shallow-coasts.html, September 13, 2020).

Arandaspis: Philippe Janvier, "Arandaspida," Tree of Life Project, January 1997 (tolweb.org/Arandaspida, September 13, 2020).

Believed to be: John Long, "The Oldest Fish in the World Lived 500 Million Years Ago," The Conversation, June 11, 2014 (theconversation.com/the-oldest-fish-in-the-world-lived-500-million-years-ago-27710, September 15, 2020).

Covered in bone-like: Palaeos, "Pteraspidomorphi: Heterostraci" (palaeos.com/vertebrates/pteraspidomorphi/heterostraci.html, September 15, 2020).

With helmets that: Philippe Janvier, "Arandaspida," Tree of Life Project, January 1997 (tolweb.org/Arandaspida, September 13, 2020).

One of the first fish: Palaeos, "Placodermi: Overview" (palaeos.com/vertebrates/placodermi/placodermi.html, September 15, 2020).

In the Gulf of California: Matt Simon, "Absurd Creature of the Week: This Parasite Eats a Fish's Tongue—And Takes Its Place," *Wired*, November 22, 2013 (www.wired.com/2013/11/absurd-creature-of-the-week-the-parasite-that-eats-and-replaces-a-fishs-tongue, September 15, 2020).

Red-Bellied Pacu: Mindy Weisberger, "'Vegetarian Piranhas' with Human-Like Teeth Found in Michigan Lakes," Live Science, August 12, 2016 (www.livescience.com/55753-fish-with-human-like-teeth-in-michigan.html, September 15, 2020).

However, if it runs: Animal Planet, "Red-Bellied Pacu," River Monsters (www.animalplanet.com/tv-shows/river-monsters/fish-guide/red-bellied-pacu, September 15, 2020).

Goblin Shark: Stephen Bizer, "*Mitsukurina owstoni*," Animal Diversity Web, 2004 (animaldiversity.org/accounts/Mitsukurina_owstoni, September 15, 2020).

The stargazer also: Casey Patton, "Northern Stargazer," Florida Museum at the University of Florida (www.floridamuseum.ufl.edu/discover-fish/species-profiles/astroscopus-guttatus, September 15, 2020).

Scientists think that: Franz Lidz, "Behold the Blobfish," *Smithsonian Magazine*, November 2015 (www.smithsonianmag.com/science-nature/behold-the-blobfish-180956967, September 15, 2020).

This fish thrives: Colin Schultz, "In Defense of the Blobfish: Why the 'World's Ugliest Animal' Isn't as Ugly as You Think It Is," *Smithsonian Magazine*, September 13, 2013 (www.smithsonianmag.com/smart-news/in-defense-of-the-blobfish-why-the-worlds-ugliest-animal-isnt-as-ugly-as-you-think-it-is-6676336, September 15, 2020).

Once removed from: Kirstin Fearnley, "Weird & Wonderful Creatures: The Blobfish," American Association for the Advancement of Science, June 1, 2016 (www.aaas.org/news/weird-wonderful-creatures-blobfish, September 20, 2020).

In fact, the blobfish: The Ugly Animal Preservation Society, "The Blobfish Needs YOU!" (uglyanimalsoc.com, September 20, 2020).

Yeah, it's really: Chesapeake Bay Program, "Skeleton Shrimp" (www.chesapeakebay.net/S=0/fieldguide/critter/skeleton_shrimp. September 13, 2020).

Actually, I'm expecting: Marine Education Society of Australasia, "Crustaceans" (www.mesa.edu.au/crustaceans/crustaceans05c.asp, September 20, 2020).

Almost all fish: NOAA, "Are All Fish Cold-Blooded?," National Ocean Service, August 8, 2019 (oceanservice.noaa.gov/facts/cold-blooded.html, September 20, 2020).

Marine mammals are: NOAA, "Marine Mammals," National Oceanic and Atmospheric Association, February 2019 (www.noaa.gov/education/resource-collections/marine-life/marine-mammals, September 19, 2020).

With a serpent-like: New Hampshire PBS, "Chlamydoselachidae—Frilled Sharks," *Wildlife Journal, Junior* (nhpbs.org/wild/chlamydoselachidae.asp, September 18, 2020).

The elusive frilled shark: Oceana, "Frilled Shark" (oceana.org/marine-life/sharks-rays/frilled-shark, September 20, 2020).

The deep-sea dragonfish: Wudan Yan, "Meet the Deep-Sea Dragonfish," *New York Times*, June 5, 2019 (www.nytimes.com/2019/06/05/science/dragonfish-teeth-transparent.html, September 21, 2020).

In this underwater: Woods Hole Oceanographic Institution, "Ocean Twilight Zone" (www.whoi.edu/know-your-ocean/ocean-topics/ocean-life/ocean-twilight-zone, September 20, 2020).

With the largest teeth: Smithsonian, "Fangtooth Fish," Ocean: Find Your Blue (ocean.si.edu/ocean-life/fish/fangtooth-fish, September 20, 2020).

With a supersize: Britannica, "Gulper," *Encyclopedia Britannica*, October 6, 2018 (www.britannica.com/animal/gulper, September 20, 2020).

Some shark teeth: Joachim Enax et al., "Structure, Composition, and Mechanical Properties of Shark Teeth," *Journal of Structural Biology* 178, no. 3 (2012): 290–99.

A group of sharks: Seattle Aquarium, "A Quiz: What Do You Call a Group of Sharks?," July 23, 2015 (www.seattleaquarium.org/ blog/quiz-what-do-you-call-group-sharks, September 20, 2020).

Tiger shark babies: Melissa Cristina Márquez, "Shark Cannibalism: It's a Thing and It Just Got Weirder," *Forbes*, December 29, 2018 (www.forbes.com/sites/melissacristinamarquez/2018/12/29/shark-cannibalism-its-a-thing-and-it-just-got-weirder/?sh=5ccbff2d45e1, September 15, 2020).

This gentle giant: National Geographic, "Whale Shark" (www.nationalgeographic.com/animals/fish/w/whale-shark, September 20, 2020).

Now here's a fish: National Geographic, "Mekong Giant Catfish" (www.nationalgeographic.com/animals/fish/m/mekong-giant-catfish, September 21, 2020).

At birth, the ocean sunfish: Oceana, "Ocean Sunfish" (oceana.org/marine-life/ocean-fishes/ocean-sunfish, September 21, 2020).

The megalodon lived: Josh Davis, "Megalodon: The Truth about the Largest Shark That Ever Lived," Natural History Museum (www.nhm.ac.uk/discover/megalodon—the-truth-about-the-largest-shark-that-ever-lived.html, September 21, 2020).

In fact, even: Jack A. Cooper et al., "Body Dimensions of the Extinct Giant Shark *Otodus megalodon*: A 2D Reconstruction," *Scientific Reports* 10 (2020) (www.nature.com/articles/s41598-020-71387-y#citeas, October 11, 2020).

This ancient shark: James "Zach" Zacharias, "Giant Megalodon Shark," Museum of Arts and Sciences, October 18, 2018 (www.moas.org/Giant-Megalodon-Shark-1-51.html, September 20, 2020).

These taste babies: NOAA, "What Is the Most Venomous Marine Animal?," National Ocean Service, April 14, 2020 (oceanservice .noaa.gov/facts/box-jellyfish.html, October 11, 2020).

Tortilla chips: Monterey Bay Aquarium, "Meet the Egg-Yolk Jelly" (www.montereybayaquarium.org/animals/animals-a-to-z/ egg-yolk-jelly, October 11, 2020).

These little thirst quenchers: NOAA, "What Are Jellyfish Made Of?," National Ocean Service, September 28, 2020 (oceanservice .noaa.gov/facts/jellyfish.html, October 11, 2020).

Our famous PB&J: Smithsonian, "Jellyfish and Comb Jellies," April 2018 (ocean.si.edu/ocean-life/invertebrates/jellyfish-and-comb-jellies, October 10, 2020).

Female lobster: New England Aquarium, "Lobsters Pee Out of . . . Where?!" *Exhibit Galleries Blog*, November 13, 2015 (galleries .neaq.org/2015/11/lobsters-pee-out-ofwhere.html, October 12, 2020).

When it comes: Katherine Harmon Courage, "Female Octopus Strangles Mate, Then Eats Him," *Scientific American*, July 22, 2014 (blogs.scientificamerican.com/octopus-chronicles/female-octopus-strangles-mate-then-eats-him, October 12, 2020).

ACTUALLY, these octodads: Truman P. Young, "Semelparity and Iteroparity," *Nature Education Knowledge* 3, no. 10 (2010) (www.nature.com/scitable/knowledge/library/semelparity-and-iteroparity-13260334, October 12, 2020).

Despite its gigantic: National Geographic, "Dumbo Octopus" (www.nationalgeographic.com/animals/invertebrates/d/dumbo-octopus, October 12, 2020).

When male and female: Liz Langley, "Romance of the Seas: Strange Mating Habits of the Seahorse," *National Geographic*, June 25, 2016 (www.nationalgeographic.com/news/2016/06/seahorse-reproduction-behavior-conservation, October 15, 2020).

The male fertilizes: National Geographic, "Seahorse Fathers Take Reins in Childbirth," June 14, 2002 (www.nationalgeographic .com/news/2002/6/seahorse-fathers-take-reins-in-childbirth, October 15, 2020).

The sea star's: Eric H. Chudler, "Invertebrate Nervous System," Neuroscience for Kids (faculty.washington.edu/chudler/invert. html, October 15, 2020).

Sea stars actually: National Geographic, "Starfish" (www.nationalgeographic.com/animals/invertebrates/group/starfish, October 15, 2020).

Sea stars have: Jane Lee, "Surprise! Scientists Find That Starfish Eyes Actually See, at Least a Little," *National Geographic*, February 7, 2018 (www.nationalgeographic.com/news/2018/2/140107-starfish-sea-star-eyes-coral-reef-ocean-animal-science, October 15, 2020).

Instead, the sea star: NOAA, "Are Starfish Really Fish?," National Ocean Service, December 4, 2020 (oceanservice.noaa.gov/ facts/starfish.html, January 11, 2021).

Tongue Twisters

With a super-sticky: National Geographic, "Giant Anteater" (www.nationalgeographic.com/animals/mammals/g/ giant-anteater, October 22, 2020).

The anteater identifies: Smithsonian, "Giant Anteater," Smithsonian's National Zoo and Conservation Biology Institute (nationalzoo.si.edu/animals/giant-anteater, October 22, 2020).

In fact, when retracted: Ed Yong, "Hummingbirds Are Where Intuition Goes to Die," *Atlantic*, November 29, 2017 (www.theatlantic.com/science/archive/2017/11/hummingbird-tongues/546992, October 22, 2020).

The chameleon's mouth: Carrie Arnold, "Chameleon Tongue Among Fastest on Earth, Video Reveals," January 5, 2016 (www .nationalgeographic.com/news/2016/01/160105-chameleons-tongue-speed-animals-science, October 22, 2020).

It's also one: Giraffe Conservation Foundation, "How Long Is a Giraffe's Tongue? What Colour Is It?" (giraffeconservation.org/ facts/how-long-is-a-giraffes-tongue-what-colour-is-it, January 20, 2020).

The tongue of: Liz Langley, "5 of Nature's Weirdest Tongues," *National Geographic*, February 24, 2014 (blog.nationalgeographic .org/2014/02/24/5-of-natures-weirdest-tongues-2, October 22, 2020).

Part V. Creepy Crawlers

The Venus flytrap: National Wildlife Federation, "Venus Flytrap" (www.nwf.org/Educational-Resources/Wildlife-Guide/Plants-and-Fungi/Venus-Flytrap, October 30, 2020).

It sucks up: San Diego Zoo, "Giant Anteater" (animals.sandiegozoo.org/animals/giant-anteater, October 22, 2020).

In fact, people in: Spencer Michels, "Bugs for Dinner?," PBS Newshour, May 7, 2012 (www.pbs.org/newshour/science/bugs-for-dinner, October 22, 2020).

For the most part: Joseph Stromberg, "6 Reasons You Should Consider Eating Insects," Vox, February 7, 2015 (www.vox.com/ 2014/4/30/5664782/insects, October 22, 2020).

Dung Beetle: Marcus Byrne, "Five Things Dung Beetles Do with a Piece of Poo," The Conversation, September 4, 2015 (theconversation.com/five-things-dung-beetles-do-with-a-piece-of-poo-47367, October 22, 2020).

That's like a human: Ella Davies, "The World's Strongest Animal Can Lift Staggering Weights," BBC, November 21, 2016 (www.bbc.com/earth/story/20161121-the-worlds-strongest-animal-can-lift-staggering-weights, October 22, 2020).

He then brings: San Diego Zoo, "Dung Beetle" (animals.sandiegozoo.org/animals/dung-beetle, October 22, 2020).

Dermestids: W. S. Cranshaw, "Dermestid Beetles (Carpet Beetles)," Colorado State University, January 2018 (extension .colostate.edu/topic-areas/insects/carpet-beetles-5-549, November 2, 2020).

Using a special: Mollie Bloudoff-Indelicato, "Flesh-Eating Beetles Explained," *National Geographic*, January 17, 2013 (blog.nationalgeographic.org/2013/01/17/flesh-eating-beetles-explained, November 2, 2020).

Jewel Wasp: Christie Wilcox, "How a Wasp Turns Cockroaches into Zombies," *Scientific American*, May 1, 2017 (www .scientificamerican.com/article/how-a-wasp-turns-cockroaches-into-zombies1, October 22, 2020).

Spittlebug's House of Bubbles: James Gorman, "Inside the Spittlebug's Bubble Home," *New York Times*, February 19, 2019 (www.nytimes.com/2019/02/19/science/spittlebugs-bubble-home.html, October 22, 2020).

Termite Towers: Lisa Margonelli, "Collective Mind in the Mound: How Do Termites Build Their Huge Structures?," *National Geographic*, August 1, 2014 (www.nationalgeographic.com/news/2014/8/140731-termites-mounds-insects-entomology-science, November 1, 2020).

This makes the hexagon: Robert Krulwich, "What Is It about Bees and Hexagons?," NPR, May 14, 2013 (www.npr.org/sections/ krulwich/2013/05/13/183704091/what-is-it-about-bees-and-hexagons, November 2, 2020).

Hercules Beetle: The National Wildlife Federation, "Rhinoceros Beetles" (www.nwf.org/Educational-Resources/Wildlife-Guide/ Invertebrates/Rhinoceros-Beetles, November 2, 2020).

Giant Long-Legged Katydid: Houston Museum of Natural Science, "Giant Long-Legged Katydid" (www.hmns.org/cockrell-butterfly-center/our-residents/giant-long-legged-katydid, November 2, 2020).

Assassin Bug: Michael Merchant, "Wheel Bugs and Other Assassin Bugs," Texas A&M Agrilife Extension (citybugs.tamu.edu/ factsheets/landscape/others/ent-1003, November 2, 2020).

You can find: Bush Heritage Australia, "Giant Burrowing Cockroaches" (www.bushheritage.org.au/species/giant-cockroaches, November 2, 2020).

At 6.5 inches: Smithsonian, "Titan Beetle," Smithsonian Snapshot, May 31, 2011 (www.si.edu/newsdesk/snapshot/titan-beetle, November 2, 2020).

Thorn Bug: F.W. Mead and Thomas R. Fasulo, "Thorn Bug," University of Florida Institute of Food and Agriculture Sciences, August 2014 (entnemdept.ufl.edu/creatures/orn/thorn_bug.htm, November 2, 2020).

Which coats my: Allyson Chiu, "Meet the 'Exploding Ant,' Which Sacrifices Itself for Its Colony," *Washington Post*, April 20, 2018 (www.washingtonpost.com/[...all]?all=news&all=morning-mix&all=wp&all=2018&all=04&all=20&all=meet-the-exploding-ant-which-sacrifices-itself-for-its-colony, November 2, 2020).

I do this weird: Charles Q. Choi, "Can a Cockroach Live without Its Head?," *Scientific American*, November 1, 2007 (www .scientificamerican.com/article/can-a-cockroach-live-without-its-he, November 2, 2020).

When I get scared: Rachel Nall, "Are Ladybugs Poisonous to People or Pets?," Healthline, May 29, 2020 (www.healthline.com/ health/are-ladybugs-poisonous, November 5, 2020).

More than forty-five thousand: National Geographic, "Spiders" (www.nationalgeographic.com/animals/invertebrates/group/ spiders, November 2, 2020).

From the 0.011-inch: Guinness World Records Limited, "World's Smallest Spider" (www.guinnessworldrecords.com/world-records/smallest-spider, November 4, 2020).

All spiders on earth: Dami Lee, "Spiders Could Theoretically Eat Every Human on Earth in a Year and That's Okay by Me," The Verge, March 28, 2017 (www.theverge.com/2017/3/28/15090046/spiders-eat-humans-consume-washington-post-study, November 4, 2020).

The female black widow: National Geographic, "Black Widow Spiders" (www.nationalgeographic.com/animals/invertebrates/group/black-widow-spiders, November 4, 2020).

Much like how: Michael Miller and Micaela Jemison, "Eight Strange but True Spider Facts," Smithsonian Stories, November 28, 2014 (www.si.edu/stories/eight-strange-true-spider-facts, November 4, 2020).

A fishing spider: Sava Ate , "Fishing Spiders: Poisonous Yet Harmless," Good Fishing Central (goodfishingcentral.com/fishing-spiders-poisonous-yet-harmless, November 4, 2020).

For its weight: Courtney Miceli, "Spider Silk Is Five Times Stronger Than Steel—Now, Scientists Know Why," *Science*, November 20, 2018 (www.sciencemag.org/news/2018/11/spider-silk-five-times-stronger-steel-now-scientists-know-why, November 4, 2020).

The male black widow: Ed Yong, "How Male Widow Spiders Avoid Being Cannibalized During Sex," *National Geographic*, September 20, 2016 (www.nationalgeographic.com/news/2016/09/animals-spiders-black-widows-cannibals, November 4, 2020).

There is a specific: Katharine Gammon, "Stinky Feet Could Pave the Way for Better Ways to Stop Mosquitoes," Phys.org, May 27, 2011 (phys.org/news/2011-05-stinky-feet-pave-ways-mosquitoes.html, November 4, 2020).

Bulldog ants can: National Geographic, "25 Cool Things about Bugs!," National Geographic Kids (www.natgeokids.com/uk/discover/animals/insects/15-facts-about-bugs, November 4, 2020).

The trap-jaw ant: Peter Aldhous, "Zoologger: The Michael Phelps of the Ant World," *New Scientist*, June 11, 2014 (www.newscientist.com/article/dn25712-zoologger-the-michael-phelps-of-the-ant-world/#ixzz6ljSUSnNX, November 4, 2020).

There are an estimated: Maggie Koerth, "The Bugs of the World Could Squish Us All," FiveThirtyEight, May 2, 2017 (fivethirtyeight.com/features/the-bugs-of-the-world-could-squish-us-all, November 5, 2020).

A whopping 98 percent: Jordan G. Teicher, "Some of the World's Coolest Animals Don't Have Spines," Slate, December 15, 2014 (slate.com/culture/2014/12/susan-middleton-photographs-marine-invertebrates-in-her-book-spineless.html, November 4, 2020).

Most invertebrates have: Understanding Evolution, "Hard Exoskeleton" (evolution.berkeley.edu/evolibrary/article/0_0_0/arthropods_06, November 5, 2020).

It even has: Maria Temming, "The Diabolical Ironclad Beetle Is Nearly Unsquishable," Science News for Students, November 23, 2020 (www.sciencenewsforstudents.org/article/diabolical-ironclad-beetle-strong-exoskeleton-nearly-unsquishable, January 11, 2021).

When it was time: Tom Harris, "How Spiders Work," How Stuff Works, August 8, 2002 (animals.howstuffworks.com/arachnids/spider2.htm, November 5, 2022).

Smell Ya Later! World's Most Stinktastic Animals

And although the: Nathaniel Scharping, "A Brief History of the Hand-standing Skunk," *Discover*, May 4, 2017 (www.discovermagazine.com/article?slug=a-brief-history-of-the-hand-standing-skunk, November 5, 2020).

The binturong: San Diego Zoo, "The Binturong" (animals.sandiegozoo.org/animals/binturong, November 5, 2020).

Here's how it works: Liz Langley, "Why This Animal's Pee Smells Like Hot Buttered Popcorn," *National Geographic*, April 23, 2016 (www.nationalgeographic.com/news/2016/04/160423-dogs-animals-pets-smell-science-scents, November 10, 2020).

In the Amazon: Elizabeth Deatrick, "The Hoatzin: Misfit, Belcher, Genetic Mystery," Audubon, October 9, 2013 (www.audubon.org/news/hoatzin, November 9, 2020).

Part VI. Awesome Amphibians

Hey guys, it's me: Amphibian Life, "How Many Eggs Do Frogs Lay? (And Why Lay So Many?)" (www.amphibianlife.com/why-do-frogs-release-such-a-large-number-of-eggs, November 9, 2020).

My father stopped: David Chapman, "Tadpole to Frog: Development Stages and Metamorphosis," *Saga Magazine*, July 8, 2020 (www.saga.co.uk/magazine/home-garden/gardening/wildlife/amphibians/the-tadpole, November 10, 2020).

Meet my spawn: Vanessa Sarasola-Puente et al., "Growth, Size and Age at Maturity of the Agile Frog (*Rana dalmatina*) in an Iberian Peninsula Population," *Zoology* (Jena) 114, no. 3 (2011) (pubmed.ncbi.nlm.nih.gov/21658922, November 10, 2020).

Poison Dart Frog: National Geographic, "Golden Poison Frog" (www.nationalgeographic.com/animals/amphibians/g/golden-poison-frog, November 15, 2020).

Surinam Toad: *National Geographic*, "Surinam Toad" (www.nationalgeographic.com/animals/amphibians/s/surinam-toad, November 15, 2020).

Emerald Glass Frog: Christina McArdle, "*Centrolene prosoblepon*," Animal Diversity Web (animaldiversity.org/accounts/Centrolene_prosoblepon, November 15, 2020).

Olm Salamander: Ed Yong, "The Olm: The blind cave salamander that lives to 100," *National Geographic*, July 20, 2010 (www.nationalgeographic.com/science/phenomena/2010/07/20/the-olm-the-blind-cave-salamander-that-lives-to-100, November 15, 2020).

Frog vs. Toad: Alina Bradford, "Facts about Frogs and Toads," Live Science, May 1, 2015 (www.livescience.com/50692-frog-facts.html, November 15, 2020).

It should come: San Diego Zoo, "Goliath Frog" (animals.sandiegozoo.org/animals/goliath-frog, November 20, 2020).

Paedophryne amanuensis: Krishna Ramanujan, "Student Researchers Help Discover World's Smallest Frog," Cornell Chronicle, March 29, 2012 (news.cornell.edu/stories/2012/03/student-researchers-help-discover-worlds-smallest-frog, November 20, 2020).

Ranging from eight to fifteen: Michelle Z. Donahue, "New Staple-Size Frog Is One of the Tiniest Ever Discovered," *National Geographic*, March 27, 2019 (www.nationalgeographic.com/animals/2019/03/smallest-frog-species-discovered-mini-mum, November 20, 2020).

Tiger salamander: Starre Vartan, "Meet the Shape-Shifting Baby Amphibians That Become Cannibals," *National Geographic*, June 26, 2019 (www.nationalgeographic.com/animals/2019/06/cannibal-morph-amphibians-adapt, November 20, 2020).

Fire salamander: Lauren Stoltz, "Venom," University of Wisconsin, April 26, 2013 (bioweb.uwlax.edu/bio203/s2013/stoltz_laur/venom.htm, November 20, 2020).

Mount Lyell salamander: John Downer, *Weird Nature: An Astonishing Exploration of Nature's Strangest Behavior* (Ontario: Firefly Books, 2002).

The four-eyed frog: Heidi Kay Smith, "Meet the Four-Eyed Frog," The Finch & Pea, February 6, 2014 (thefinchandpea.com/2014/02/06/meet-the-four-eyed-frog, November 20, 2020).

The wood frog: National Park Service, "Wood Frog," Gates of the Arctic, December 16, 2020 (www.nps.gov/gaar/learn/nature/wood-frog-page-1.htm, January 11, 2021).

Wallace's flying frog: *National Geographic*, "Wallace's Flying Frog" (www.nationalgeographic.com/animals/amphibians/w/wallaces-flying-frog, November 12, 2020).

The word amphibian: Biodiversity Institute of Ontario, "Amphibian," Encyclopedia of Life, May 24, 2012 (eol.org/docs/discover/amphibians, January 11, 2021).

Mobile Homes

The two separate pieces: James MacDonald, "Turtle Shells: More Than Meets the Eye," JStor Daily, September 11, 2015 (daily.jstor.org/turtle-shells-meets-eye, November 20, 2020).

Also, I'm nocturnal: G. W. Dekle and T. R. Fasulo, "Brown Garden Snail," University of Florida Institute of Food and Agricultural Sciences, July 2014 (entnemdept.ufl.edu/creatures/misc/gastro/brown_garden_snail.htm, November 21, 2020).

Talk about a mobile: Darryl Fears, "This Invasive Giant Snail Is Spreading in Florida," *Washington Post*, July 10, 2015 (www.washingtonpost.com/news/energy-environment/wp/2015/07/10/giant-land-snails-are-on-the-move-and-a-nasty-parasite-is-riding-them-like-a-bus, November 21, 2020).

Three-banded armadillo: *National Geographic*, "Armadillos" (www.nationalgeographic.com/animals/mammals/group/armadillos, November 21, 2020).

Part VII. Generation Conservation

In 2011, a group of biologists: Camilo Mora et al., "How Many Species Are There on Earth and in the Ocean?" *PLOS Biology* 9, no. 8 (2011) (www.journals.plos.org/plosbiology/article?id=10.1371/journal.pbio.1001127, April 8. 2021).

identified about 1.2 million: Fred Pearce, "Global Extinction Rates: Why Do Estimates Vary So Wildly?" Yale Environment 360, August 17, 2015 (www. e360.yale.edu/features/global_extinction_rates_why_do_estimates_vary_so_wildly, April 8, 2021).

PHOTO CREDITS

DanielaAgius/iStockphoto.com: 187 (bottom)

Ale-ks/iStock/Getty Images: 3 (top image, second from bottom right), 175 (bottom)

ALEAIMAGE/iStock/Getty Images: 116

Anest/Shutterstock: 174 (top)

Antagain/iStock/Getty Images Plus/Getty Images: 51 (bottom), 175 (top)

Arco Images GmbH/TUNS/Alamy: 102 (top)

CK Bangkok Photography/Shutterstock: 156

Jeff Banke/Shutterstock: 186 (bottom)

Mark Beckwith/Shutterstock: 105

bennytrapp/Adobe Stock: 91

Archana Bhartia/Hemera/Getty Images: 128 (right)

Lukas Blazek/Dreamstime: 93 (bottom)

BVDC/Fotolia: 60 (bottom)

Lynn Carlson/EyeEm/Getty Images: 173

John Carnemolla/Shutterstock: 75 (bottom), 79 (left)

Cathy Withers-Clarke/Shutterstock: 159

CMCD/Photodisc/Getty Images: 115 (bottom)

JohannesCompaan/E+/Getty Images: 95 (middle)

covenant/Shutterstock: 75 (middle right)

Jessica Lynn Culver/Moment Open/Getty Images: 99 (top)

Lee Dalton/Alamy: 85 (left)

Damsea/Shutterstock: 39, 106 (top)

Rob Daugherty–RobsWildlife.com/Flickr/Getty Images: 98 (bottom)

Tim Davis/Corbis: 150 (bottom)

Deaddogdodge/Dreamstime: 99 (second from top)

Alexandre Fagundes De Fagundes/Dreamstime: 150 (top)

Dominique de La Croix/Shutterstock: 30

Carol Dembinsky/Dembinsky Photo Associates/Alamy: 155 (top)

Digital Vision/Getty Images: 3 (top image, second from left), 37 (top), 99 (bottom)

Georgette Douwma/Photodisc/Getty Images: 121

Sam Dudgeon/Houghton Mifflin Harcourt: 3 (top image, top right), 19, (top left), 36, 100 (top)

EcoView/Fotolia: 56

Dario Egidi/iStockphoto.com: 3 (top image, second from bottom left)

Dirk Ercken/Alamy: 189

Cedric Favero/Moment Open/Getty Images: 114 (right)

Melinda Fawver/Shutterstock: 180 (bottom)

Michael Flippo/Fotolia: 98 (middle)

Greg Forcey/Alamy: 93 (top)

Four Oaks/Shutterstock: 158

Rodrigo Friscione/Cultura/Getty Images: 51 (second from bottom), 131 (bottom right)

Gaertner/Alamy: 103

GlobalP/iStockphoto.com: 150 (middle)

Gennady Grechishkin/Shutterstock: 3 (top image, second from right)

James Bloor Griffiths/Shutterstock: 37 (bottom)

James Gritz/Photodisc/Getty Images: 43

Shane Gross/Shutterstock: 131 (middle right)

Aleksandar Grozdanovski/Shutterstock: 199 (top)

harlequinarcher/Fotolia: 57 (middle)

Hawaiian/iStockphoto.com: 54 (top left), 55 (bottom)

Shawn Hempel/Shutterstock: 22, 35 (center)

Andrew_Howe/iStockphoto.com: 83 (top)

Vitalii Hulai/Shutterstock: 197 (bottom)

inhauscreative/E+/Getty Images: 199 (bottom)

irakite/iStock/Getty Images: 104 (bottom), 151

Eric Isselee/Shutterstock: 20, 75 (top), 85 (right), 112 (middle), 180 (top), 187 (top)

Jodi Jacobson/E+/Getty Images: 205 (middle)

jaroslava V/Shutterstock: 106 (bottom)

joebelanger/iStock/Getty Images: 138

johan63/iStock/Getty Images: 107

INDEX

THE THANK-YOU PAGE

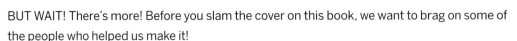

BUT WAIT! There's more! Before you slam the cover on this book, we want to brag on some of the people who helped us make it!

First, we'd like to thank our incredible and incredibly funny illustrators, Jack Teagle and Mike Centeno. We'd also like to thank our wonderful designers, Samira Iravani and Abby Dening, and colorist Nakata Whittle. Every draft of your illustrations and design felt like a gift.

Major high-fives to our friend and longtime collaborator Thomas van Kalken for helping us scheme, research, and imagine new ways to present the animals in this book. If you could only hear all the laughs that are tucked into these pages!

We also owe a huge heap of gratitude to our diligent fact checkers, Jessica Boddy and Jen Monnier. Because of them, you can rest assured that this book is *not* full of a bunch of nonsense that we totally made up ourselves. Everything in here is both ridiculous AND true!

We'd also like to send a big bouquet of THANK-YOUs to our amazing and brilliant editor, Amy Cloud, who has been our most enthusiastic cheerleader from day one. We love you, Amy!

And hats off to the teams at Clarion Books and HarperCollins Publishers for helping to bring this book to your hands: Mary Magrisso, Megan Gendell, Erika West, Susan Bishansky, Melissa Cicchitelli, Julie Yeater, Lisa DiSarro, and Tara Shanahan.

Please stand back while we dump a big bunch of gratitude on our literary agent, Steven Malk, for his guidance, encouragement, and kindness from the very beginning.

Big hugs and lots of appreciation to our families for their love and patience as we corralled the wild animals on these pages: our spouses, Ryan and Hannah, and our wild kids, Rhett, Birdie, Henry, and Bram (who provided us with more inspiration than they know).

Finally, while this book might be for your eyeballs, our *Wow in the World* podcast is for your earballs! And we'd like to thank our wildly talented team at Tinkercast, who help to make everything you see and hear from us possible: Jed Anderson, Anna Zagorski, Henry Moskal, Rebecca Caban, Kit Ballenger, Madeline Bender, Jason Rabinowitz, Jacob Stein, and, of course, our #1 partner in *Wow,* Meredith Halpern-Ranzer.

Wait . . . are we missing anyone? Oh, that's right, YOU! THANK YOU! A book isn't officially a book until it has someone to read it, so it sure is nice of you to help us complete the process. We hope you have as much fun reading it as we did writing it! You're the best. Now go ahead, slam this thing shut and get outside to find some WOW and WILD in your world! —M.T. & G.R.